THE

HOUSE OF SCINDEA

THE HOUSE OF SCINDEA

A SKETCH

JOHN HOPE

GYAN

Published by

GYAN

Gyan Publishing House
5, Ansari Road
Daryaganj, New Delhi-110002
Phone: 011-47034999, 9811692060
E-mail: books@gyanbooks.com

Distribution Network
gyanbooks.com
India, USA, Canada, UK, Australia, France

ISBN: 978-81-212-9138-5 (PB)
First Published, 1863

2nd Impression 2023

Printed at: Gyan Press, Delhi.

THE HOUSE OF SCINDEA
AUTHOR: JOHN HOPE

THE HOUSE OF SCINDEA.

THE

HOUSE OF SCINDEA:

A SKETCH.

BY JOHN HOPE,

LATE SUPERINTENDING SURGEON OF SCINDEA'S CONTINGENT, AND SURGEON TO THE COURT OF GWALIOR.

LONDON:
LONGMAN, GREEN, LONGMAN, ROBERTS, & GREEN.
1863.

THE

HOUSE OF SCINDEA.

We have no right to seize Scinde, yet we shall do so—and a very advantageous, useful, humane piece of RASCALITY *it will be.*

SIR CHARLES NAPIER.

NEITHER the similarity of the names Scinde and Scindea, nor the quotation which heads this page, will, we trust, mislead those of our readers who are not very well acquainted with the localities of India. We are not going to follow the beaten path that directs our way to Hydrabad on the Indus. We proceed to Gwalior in Central India, intending to relate occurrences which took place there; and should our narrative prove little gratifying, on the whole, to the pride and sense of honour of Englishmen, it will at least have the merit of being substantially true; and it may possibly have this further claim on the sympathy of our readers, that, like comedies on the stage, it ends by the last of its heroes, Gyajea Scindea, turning out a very fine character, — a youth of courage and ability, devoted to the interests of the British Government.

We may premise that since the great mutinies, and, beyond all doubt, in consequence of them, the public opinion of England has taken a great turn in respect to our relations with the Princes of India. In the days of annexation it was the fashion to decry Native Governments; and Secretaries in Calcutta delighted to descant on the great iniquities of the Native Rulers, and to shower the most extravagant praise on the British administration, which they designated, in their stereotyped phraseology, 'a mild and paternal sway.' That was sheer diplomatic cant. The real and only aim of these officials was to enlarge our dominions, to increase patronage, and to add more regiments to our already enormous sepoy-army; and the self-imposed task of these men and their masters, the Governors-General, was to effect their unrighteous purpose with as little damage to their reputation as possible. Not to go further back than the time of the late Lord Dalhousie—himself, in some respects, the most brilliant Governor-General since the time of Lord Wellesley—we find that he made it 'the glory and the boast' of his remarkable administration, that, in seven years, he had annexed 'four splendid Provinces' to the empire! But, thanks to

Lord Stanley, that policy, if it has not passed away for ever, has received a check; and we now solemnly engage, in the name of Her Majesty the Queen of England, to govern India with justice to all, and with honest dealing towards the landed aristocracy and the Princes of the country; and to play in future the part of the dog that protects the sheep rather than, as hitherto, that of the wolf that devours them.

We may observe, in this place, that there is not a more general, and certainly not a pleasanter illusion among persons who never resided in India than that the 180 millions who inhabit the immense plains between the Himalayah mountains and Cape Comorin are largely impressed with the conviction that the Government of Great Britain in India is not only paternal and magnanimous, but that it is felt and recognised as the only government, within that wide territory, where every wrong can be redressed; where tortures, such as are alleged to be commonly practised by native rulers, have long ceased; where the peasantry especially is contented; and where 'the greatest happiness of the greatest number' is the chief object of its power. Drawbacks of course, those enthusiasts say, there must be. Certain clans are, by long habit, untractable. The highest classes have no public service to obtain under English sway. The great landed-interest, as we understand the term in England, it is acknowledged, has no particular love to bestow on us; but, despite these exceptional facts as they are called, the untravelled Englishman, unruffled by the lesson which the mutinies of 1857 taught, puts his hands into his pockets and feels proudly conscious that the masses are perfectly satisfied and even charmed with the destiny which placed them under the dominion of Queen Victoria. Nor is this illusion altogether inexplicable. If we turn to France we find that, in this present day, a large proportion of its people possess the inward sense amounting to absolute certainty, that Napoleon won the battle of Waterloo; and we further know, that a host of persons of the Roman Catholic persuasion believe, that the tiny pieces of wood, which the priests of Spain and Italy give away unsparingly at Easter, are really atoms of the true Cross of our Saviour. The explanation in these instances is the same, and it is that the wish is father to the thought.

It is not our desire to sweep away, if we could, this Indian illusion, or other fallacies of the kind which we could mention. What we hope is, that our readers will not put down this little sketch of affairs at a native court, and lift up their hands with horror, if we affirm that we have found much to admire and very little to detest in the administration of public affairs at Gwalior. Such is our conviction, knowing well that if the people of India—the 180 millions—could go to the poll on a choice of governments, an almost countless majority would prefer a native one, (though, as a matter of course, it preyed extensively upon their industry and wealth), to one which was ever supervising and controlling every act of their public life, and haunting them with the vision of an English court of law. The temperament of the people is not quite understood. If we take up a book on Italy, we are sure to find that it is 'the land of the sun, and of ardent imaginations.' India, too, is 'the land of the sun,' but the people are the impersonation of apathy; their entire exemption from passion being, indeed, the secret of our retention of the Empire. Who were the leaders of the mutineers at Delhi? Old and worn-out Subadars, who had risen to their rank by the gradation system, just as General Hewett, who commanded at Meerut, had done; men one step from the invalid establishment and two from the grave; not men who had a spark of the daring and fire of a Garabaldi, or the energy of that Jeswunt Sing who attracted the admiration of the Eastern world in the early period of Aurungzebe's reign.

There are many reasons why the British Government is not liked. To take a single instance: we need only remark that if there be a sentiment deeply rooted in the hearts of the people, it is their aversion to a race that eats the flesh of cows and pigs. They care absolutely nothing about our forms of faith—very many question if we have any religious faith at all. The splendid structures of former rulers are seen to decay under us, and there is no complaining. So long as their home rights, their caste and their religion, are tolerated, public feeling for or against any existing government, never manifests itself. All is repose; and it is this harmonious whole which is considered by the illusionists in England as a proof of universal loyalty and contentment; but there is still one dark spot in our character—we are outcasts, and we will not say hated—but regarded without affection for our uncleanness.

Well would it be if there were no other cause for dissatisfaction. Is there a single official in India who would venture to assert that the administration of justice, as conducted in that country, is the same as it is represented to be in England by one of our most eminent judges, Sir William Erle, 'the highest of all human interests?' We make no allusion to the courts of law in the great seaport towns of Calcutta, Madras, and Bombay, which very little concern the natives. We speak of Mofussil justice, such as is meted out throughout the land by judges in the enjoyment of a salary of 3,000*l.* a year, but whose legal attainments do not extend beyond the sections to be found in the Civil and Criminal Procedure Code—men from Hayleybury and the competitive examination rooms. Below them sit the native bar, a set of land-sharks; then we have the Nazir, or sheriff; the Thannadar, or inspector of police; and lastly the Burkundanze, or policeman. Perhaps it will amuse the reader to peruse 'a case' which has been reported by no less a personage than the late Sir William Sleeman:—

'A robbery affords a rich harvest. Some article of stolen property is found in one man's house, and by a little legerdemain it is conveyed to that of another, both of whom are made to pay liberally; the man robbed also pays, and all the members of the village community are made to do the same. They are all called to the court of the Thannadar to give evidence as to what they have seen or heard regarding either the fact, or the persons in the remotest degree connected with it—as to the arrests of the supposed offenders—the search of their house—the character of their grandmothers and grandfathers; and they are told, that they are to be sent to the magistrate a hundred miles distant, and there made to stand at the door among 150 pairs of shoes,' (all natives who attend our courts of law are made to leave their shoes at the outer door) 'till his Excellency the Nazir, the sheriff of the court, may be pleased to announce them to his Highness the magistrate, which of course he will not do without a consideration. To escape these threatened evils they pay handsomely, and depart in peace. The Thannadar reports that an attempt to rob a house, by persons unknown, had been defeated by his exertions and the good fortune of the magistrate, and sends a liberal share of the spoil to those who are to read his report to that functionary. This goes on more or less in every district, but more especially in those where the magistrate happens to be a man of violent temper, who is always surrounded by knaves, because natives who have any regard for their character will not approach him;—or a weak good-natured man, easily made to believe anything, and managed by favourites;—or one too fond of field sports or of his own ease.'

We shall give one more illustration of 'justice in

the Mofussil,' and then contrast it with the course of procedure at Gwalior. It is taken from 'The Friend of India,' a newspaper of the largest circulation, and conducted by the best talent in India. The case is still *sub judice* by the supreme government, and therefore we suppress the name of the station, though 'The Friend of India' uses no such delicacy:—

'A case has come under our notice of so monstrous a character, that we hesitate to believe there is an English judge, even in India, of whom the story is true. The facts demand strict and immediate enquiry on the part of the North-West Government. The judge of Ghazeepore, in a civil case brought in appeal before him, suspects a document. Under these circumstances there are by law two courses. One is, under section 171 of the Criminal Procedure Code, to make the case over to the magistrate for enquiry; the other, under section 173, to complete the investigation himself. In either case a complete enquiry, comprising the defence of the prisoner, is indispensable before he is committed to the Sessions Court. With the law staring him in the face, the judge neither remits the case for enquiry to the magistrate nor completes it himself, but at once orders the magistrate to send the case to the sessions, so that, in fact, a commitment to the Sessions Court takes place, without any preliminary trial at all. When the sessions judge gets the case before him, he literally sentences the prisoner to ten years' imprisonment, without taking his defence before the Sessions Court at all. Before doing this, the prisoner, having remonstrated against the procedure of the judge in refusing to record answers favourable to him, and showing the witness what he (the judge) wished him to record, the judge reviled the prisoner from the bench, calling him "Haramzadah, Badmashsee." * The Sudder sends the case back for the prisoner's defence to be taken. The poor wretch, being considerably depressed and bewildered after four months' imprisonment, brings in a written memorandum to refresh his memory, and represents that his mind is not in such a state as to enable him to make a clear defence without referring to this. He begins to give his defence, the judge flies into a rage, makes his chuprasses write the memorandum, and on the pretext that a prisoner ought not to have time to write, orders an enquiry into the circumstance by the magistrate, and sends the case up again without a defence. There are

* Bastard! Robber!

other facts in the case, but these will be sufficient. The sentence, in a case which at the worst, if proved, possesses no features of aggravation, is scandalously vindictive—ten years' rigorous imprisonment, 2,000 rs. fine, and the confiscation during the whole term of the prisoner's entire property, movable and immovable, without any provision being made for his children or household. The case has naturally caused a great sensation throughout the district.'

It is to be hoped that if any enthusiast of 'British rule at any price' has read this page, he is coming, however slowly, to perceive that it is not in our law courts in India that the goddess of Justice would take especial pride in spreading out her wings. In Scindea's country there are no courts of law; and justice, if it cost anything at all, is, what it ought to be, cheap and at every man's door. Let us suppose that Buxoo has a grievance against Ramkissen. He does not go to a solicitor to get him to file a bill and to lodge a retainer for the services of a Malins or a Cairns of the native bar. He proceeds to the *Potail*, or head man of his village, with his complaint, who directs a *punchayut* to assemble, by whom investigation is made, and redress given on the spot. *Punchayut* signifies 'a court of five persons,' and it is, beyond all question, regarded as the *magna charta* of the millions, though, from deference to English prejudices and patronage, it is denied, unhappily, to the 180 millions who are under our sway. In that court is no evidence of inferiority of race exhibited by suitors walking barefoot, whilst the high-salaried judge has his own boots resting, perhaps, on the very table of the justice-hall itself; no Hayleybury law to mystify Buxoo; no calling of foul names from the judgment-seat; no highnesses or excellencies; and, worse than all, no black Bumbles to descant on their exertions, and to flatter the great functionaries. All these are signs of civilisation which at present lie far beyond the vision of the Mahrattas. Their's is a degenerate State where a man can get a sort of equity which satisfies though it be not judicial; which costs nothing, and which is unattended with vexatious delays.

But now to our narrative. That we may be better understood, we propose to begin with a short history of the country and the dynasty of Scindea. The country is in length rather more than 300 miles, and extends almost from the city of Agra, in the north-west presidency, to Bombay in the south. Its breadth is very unequal. In its general aspect it differs little from the rest of the vast plains of India. Whilst the Prince and the Court are Mahrattas, the people themselves are Rajpoots and Jauts, and differ therefore from their rulers in race, though not in religion; but it is a very remarkable fact, and one that explains our own wonderful ascendency over the people of India, that a foreign yoke is not felt as an additional weight to the bondage under which, more or less, they all necessarily labour. As the country is, on the whole, a poor one, and, as it has little trade, except in opium and corn, and no manufactures at all worthy of the name (although the shawls of Boorhampoor are very highly valued by natives), it never could be regarded as a prey worthy of much consideration to the British Government, except for the great natural advantages of its situation. It connects Agra with Bombay. So long as it belonged to Scindea, it was said to be a perpetual obstacle to quick and direct communication between upper India and England, until the day came when, by the overthrow of the Ameers of Scinde, through a 'humane piece of rascality,' as cited at the head of this book, the Indus was thrown open to our steamers. The great problem, therefore, was to discover how this coveted country might fall into our grasp, when its rulers observed, even more than many other chieftains, those amenities which Oriental diplomacy has rendered so amusing to John Bull at home. We shall show, by and by, how the solution of this problem was attempted by two of our Governors-General unsuccessfully, as good luck would have it; but we will ask the attention of our readers, first of all, to a rapid notice of the House of Scindea.

In the time of the Peishwas, the rulers of the Dekkan, when all India was overrun by war, and the English were struggling for new, ere they were sure of holding their own moderate possessions, there lived a man named Mahdajee Scindea, who, if not a great man, was, with the exception of his signal defeat at the memorable battle of Pâniput, at least a very successful man. His father, Ranojee Scindea, held, at the Court of Poona the office of slipper-bearer to the Peishwa (the great-grandfather of the scoundrel Nana Sahib), a position in the scale of servitors on a par, perhaps, with that of a Page of Honour at Windsor. But the drum which beat the little Mahratta horsemen to arms, had a charm and a significance in the mind of the slipper-bearer, and roused him from the luxurious indolence of an Oriental palace life. He entered the army, and died a distinguished general. His son, Mahdajee Scindea, following up the good fortune of his father, won a throne; and his heir, at this day, is recognised as an independent prince by the British Government. If the reader should desire to peruse the history of the career of the daring and unscrupulous Mahdajee, we refer him to Malcolm's admirable 'Memoirs of Central India.' It will be enough here to remark that, like other great conquerors in those times, he went in for an immense stake in battles, plundered whole provinces, and slaughtered much people; and, to these common crimes of victors, added one that constituted the peculiar mode of warfare of the Mahrattas, which was to spread desolation, whether avoidable or not, wherever Mahratta armies proceeded. His conquests, therefore, whilst for a long time they ruined the country which he and his heirs were destined to rule, gained no sympathy amongst any of the races of India, but gave just reason for the deep-rooted hatred, and even horror, which the very mention of the name of the Mahratta excited in the earlier period of the Scindea dynasty. Mahdajee died in 1794, and his name is commemorated at Gwalior to the present day, more, however, with reference to a very remarkable incident in his earlier career than by reason of his great successes as a warrior. After the battle of Pâniput, when his whole army fled in great disorder, Mahdajee, mounted on a splendid charger, was observed by an Affghan to be making his escape. The Affghan, armed to the teeth, but riding merely a sturdy hill pony, pursued him. As often as Scindea turned round, so often was he doomed to see his enemy close behind him. Presently his charger fell into a ditch, when the Mahomedan slashed at Scindea with his sword and cut open his knee; and perceiving a beautiful pearl necklace under his quilted coat, dismounted and seized it, then spat on his enemy's face and left him to die. Fortunately, Scindea was not known to his foe, or his head would have been cut off and carried in triumph to the Affghan sovereign. Some kind Samaritan happening to pass by, saved his life. Nothing so much gratified Mahdajee in the latter period of his life as the recital of this tale. As an old retired fox-hunter cannot resist the pleasure of talking over some celebrated run with 'the Squire' in years gone by; so it is said of Mahdajee, that, in his old age, he delighted to relate this hair-breadth escape, and used to tell his admiring courtiers that he rarely had a disturbing dream without seeing in it the ruthless savage on the sturdy hill pony.

Dowlut Rao Scindea, an adopted son, succeeded the founder of his House. By this time the British power had become paramount in India, and the new prince, a man of moderate capacity, was compelled by us to give up a course of pillage and conquests. Lord Wellesley drew up a treaty, the famous one of Bassain, than which none ever had a more withering influence upon the great chiefs of the country. By its terms the British Government, to avoid all semblance of partiality, determined that actual possessors at that date, 1803, should be regarded as rightful possessors, thus erecting for the numerous class of petty chiefs, the feudal lords of the country, that solid and lasting foundation for their possessions which had never existed before. The effect which this master-stroke of policy gradually produced in the character of the native princes it is impossible to estimate fully. Thirty years afterwards, search where you would within the circle of India as then formed, no Mahdajee Scindea, Jeswunt Rao Holkar, or Ameer Khan, generals of the soil, could anywhere be found. The greatest civilian whom the civil service of India ever reared, Sir John Lawrence, was asked one day by one of his earliest friends, to what circumstance the suppression of the frightful mutinies of 1857 was to be chiefly ascribed. His answer was, 'To a succession of miracles, but if to one circumstance more than another, to the fact that, amongst a hundred-and-fifty thousand mutineers, there was not a general. If,' added that great man, 'they had had *half* a general, we must have lost India.' By putting an end to military enterprises, Lord Wellesley destroyed the school for native generals. The consequence is, the descendants of the old Indian warriors, the present princes, have no martial disposition; but, with rare exceptions, pass their days amongst the females of the zenanah, or, bespangled with splendid ornaments, that are becoming in our eyes only to women, while away their time listening to the monotonous sound of the tom-tom. But Dowlut Rao, if he could make no raids, joined in no such orgies as take place behind the eastern purdah. He had married the Baiza Bye, the most remarkable woman of the day. His boast was (and a most singular one it is, when we remember the low esteem in which women are held in all eastern countries), that he never undertook an affair of importance without consulting her. Nevertheless, though brought up amidst the tumults of war, and counselled by an ambitious wife, he also, by degrees, subsided into a common-place ruler, and just before his death, having no son, adopted Junkojee Scindea, then an infant, and appointed his talented widow Regent of Gwalior during the minority.

It was during the regency of this lady that our wars with the Burmese and the usurper of Bhurtpoor took place—wars which cleared the treasury of

Calcutta of the immense surplus cash which the frugal administration of the Marquis of Hastings had amassed. To get money somewhere and somehow was a necessity which the Governor-General, Lord Amherst, felt, admitted of no delay. The King of Oude could not be applied to again. He had lent a few millions, five or six, and had been paid off with a strip of territory taken from Nepaul. 'Suppose,' said a Calcutta magnate, 'we try what Scindea will do. The Mahrattas are a singularly penurious race, and the coffers of their chief are believed to be well filled with rupees—two, or may be three crores buried in the palace; and who can say that the Baiza Bye would be indifferent to the *éclât* of lending the great Company Bahadoor a paltry million?' The shrewd idea was acted on. Colonel Stewart, a very able diplomatist, was the Resident at the Court of Gwalior, and to him was confidentially entrusted the delicate task of pumping—we beg pardon for the vulgarism—her Royal Highness. Now, we do not doubt that some extremely watchful game-keeper has caught a weasel very fast asleep, although the fact is not recorded in any known work on Natural History; but we very much question if any Resident at her court ever found the Baiza Bye napping. She was a true Asiatic woman, 'and something more;'—crafty, false, intriguing, vigilant; 'the something more' being that she had not, it was said, a single amiable weakness. By some means or other, this artful personage got scent of the intention to borrow, and naturally enough became awakened to a sense of the danger. She hastily dispatched a favourite, one Dada Khasgeewalla—of whom we shall hear more by and by—to the Colonel, to ask him if he thought, her troops being mutinous on account of not getting their pay, the British government could be persuaded to lend her a million? Here was a singular coincidence certainly, and one that took the wind completely out of the sails of the gallant Resident. We may suppose, without drawing largely on the imagination, that Colonel Stewart wrote to his lordship, Lord Amherst, expressing his deep concern and surprise—we *know* that the Dada did surprise him—to find that Her Highness herself was in great want of money. 'Indeed, her minister has just been here to ask me if the British government could lend her a million!' Some time after this, the astute Dada suggested to his mistress that Junkojee Scindea, the minor, was getting near his majority, and that, if she propitiated the paramount power by a loan, she might be allowed to govern during her life. She perceived the force of that suggestion, and lent the money. She even did more;—she thoroughly enjoyed the cruel joke which she had successfully practised on the credulity of the Resident, of whom it was said that he never alluded to the Baiza Bye's artifice without entirely forgetting the dignified composure which was habitual to him. But the joke was some time afterwards turned against her Highness, and we confess that we cannot give currency to the way in which it was done without sincere concern. It happened that many years before this loan affair, a transaction had occurred between our government and one of the Scindeas, in respect of which the former advanced a claim to a quarter of a million sterling, and the latter repudiated the debt. What the transaction was, or when it occurred, we cannot precisely say, but it was a very old dispute, never settled, but suffered to die out, consigned by a continuous silence to the limbo of the past. However, time passed on, a new Governor-General came to India, and another Resident went to Gwalior. The Calcutta treasury was filling through the blessings of peace, and the Baiza Bye was to be paid. 'In full,' says John Bull, 'of course.' No! Only three quarters of a million,' say the authorities in Calcutta, 'as we have a little claim for the other quarter.'

Imagine the penurious woman stunned by such an answer! She was told that her money, thus mulcted, was in the treasury at Benares, that interest on it was stopped, and that she might send for it when she pleased. We know that the acting Resident, Colonel Fielding, incurred much displeasure at head-quarters for daring to urge, as a matter of common fairness and justice, the payment in full. As it is, we mention the circumstance sorely against our will, and advisedly abstain from all comment.

We now come to a period when it was hoped by the Governor-General and other officials in Calcutta, that the Gwalior State would fall an easy victim to the iniquitous system of annexation; and that it did not fall, is solely ascribable to the lofty sense of honour of Mr. Cavendish, the Resident at Scindea's capital. The incident which we are about to relate establishes another fact, viz., that things were done by high personages in Calcutta which were not fully chronicled, as they ought to have been, for the information of the Court of Directors. In 1833, Junkojee Scindea came of age, and was entitled to be placed on the guddee, or silken cushion; a ceremonial which, after the Mahratta fashion, is tantamount to a coronation with us. But nothing could be more opposed to the will or intention of the Baiza

Bye, than the relinquishment of the reins of power. This woman was a person of the most undaunted courage, whilst the young prince, wickedly enervated in the zenanah, with the view to render him unfit to govern, was a well-intentioned, good-looking, but timid youth. Arbitrary government, however, is nowhere popular; and the Bye, an unmitigated despot, was exceedingly unpopular. Her discernment soon detected the sign that her regency was drawing to an end. It may be amusing to some of our readers to be told the sure indication of a coming downfall at an eastern court. The Derbys, Palmerstons, and Russells of the Durbar, when sent for to advise, are simultaneously kept at home by some sudden indisposition. It was so in this case. Her most devoted ministers, her commandants of brigades, even the Brahmins, were all confined to their houses by distressing catarrhs. They would fain attend, but sickness has seized them. When this sign appears in the court of a native prince, the time for packing has arrived. A tumult then followed; and one Hookum Sing, a daring Sepoy, under cover of the darkness of the night, scaled, by means of a ladder, the wall of the bedroom in which the young Maharajah was confined, and, aided possibly by some friendly nymph within, entered the chamber and dragged out of the window the affrighted prince, who anticipated nothing less fearful than instant assassination. The Sepoy conveyed him to the Lushkur, a military camp of twenty thousand men, adjoining which, or rather in which, the palace of Scindea stands. 'The revolution,' as it was called, was now virtually effected. On hearing these tidings, the regent, with all her retinue, fled from the palace, and, narrowly escaping with her life, sought shelter in the British territories. Of course there were factions in the capital. There were, as with us, on a change of ministry, the ins and the outs. It was during this natural ferment at the seat of government that the Governor-General, Lord William Bentinck, was so ill advised as to allow the Baiza Bye to take up her permanent residence on the border of Scindea's frontier, where, herself secure from all possible attacks by the inviolability of the English soil she occupied, she could keep alive the troubles of the capital she had been compelled to leave. The disappointed 'Horsmans' among the Brahmins soon 'went over' to her camp, and she began to think she could make head once more against her adopted and, by her, despised son. An Eurasian general, the Napier of the Gwalior army, quitted the city with fifteen hundred men, a month afterwards, avowedly to join the Bye at Agra. A report was industriously spread through Gwalior by her emissaries that Lord William Bentinck secretly favoured her cause. The young Maharajah, who was greatly disquieted, remonstrated against the unfairness of his lordship, in allowing her highness to reside near the frontier, and Mr. Cavendish, the Resident, supported his representations with great spirit, but all to no purpose; the Governor-General declaring the Bye's perfect right to reside wherever and to do whatever she pleased. The consequence was, that every day revealed the hatching of some new conspiracy in the capital, and the condition of the new ministry may be imagined when we state that the Sepoy, Hookum Sing, the hero of the scaling ladder, proceeded to the Durbar, where a cabinet of high caste Brahmins was sitting, and, in the presence of the young prince, took off his shoe and soundly thrashed every one of the ministers. The mere semblance of a government scarcely remained; the Maharajah insulted, his ministers buffeted in his presence, the principal military officers imprisoned by their own men! Poor Junkojee Scindea began now to perceive the truth of the well-known saying of our great poet, that—

> Uneasy lies the head that wears a crown.

But if these dangers surrounded him in his Capital, he was threatened with no less danger from the council of Calcutta. Secret deliberations were there being held, with a view to discover what profit could be made out of the troubles of this weak but most faithful young prince. A demi-official letter,—and what is a demi-official letter? the reader may ask. Well, it is a letter of a mongrel kind,—half private, half official; authoritative if needed by events, mystic if the job is too bad to be proclaimed. One of the best acts of Lord Ellenborough was to extinguish this common and most nefarious mode of the epistolary part of government. A demi-official letter was written to the Resident, by the chief Secretary of the Foreign department, desiring him to learn, at a private interview, by way of a feeler, if the Maharajah, encircled as he was by serious troubles—troubles mainly caused by our government—would like to resign; assigning over the country to the British government, and receiving a handsome pension, which would be paid out of his own revenues. There can be very little doubt that this demi-official document was of the genus *mystic*, and that no copy of it can now be found among the archives pertaining to India. Mr. Cavendish, than whom no Englishman ever attained a greater ascendancy over the minds of the natives with whom he had concern, declined to make such a suggestion, and his answer threw a damp upon the hopes of the annexationists. It was upon the advice of this able and honourable political officer that the young Maharajah took heart, expelled the mal-contents (among whom was Hookum Sing), removed the incompetent Brahmin administrators, and, wisest act of all, placed, for the first time since the family of Scindea ruled the country, the command of his somewhat mutinous army in the hands of a Christian, the celebrated Jean Baptiste; measures which restored peace, and maintained it during the whole of Junkojee Scindea's reign. This dedication of his talents to securing the quiet of the capital and the improvement of the country, has rendered the name of 'Cavendish' famous in the state to this day. But when his refusal to put the question of the pension reached Calcutta, and it was known there that all tumult had passed away, intense was the displeasure in all quarters. The government officials were of course extremely angry. The press, almost entirely supported by the civil and military services which are immensely benefited by annexation, was very abusive. Presently another demi-official letter arrived; this time from the Deputy Secretary of the Foreign department—a '*mystic*' one we may be quite sure—strongly expostulating with Mr. Cavendish upon his proceedings, and concluding with this significant remark:—'You have thus allowed a favourable chance to escape of connecting the Agra to the Bombay presidency.' Of course the Resident's doom was fixed, though not just then declared. A few months afterwards, the Governor-General gratified his feelings of resentment by removing Mr. Cavendish to another native court. If he had connected the two presidencies, there is no kind of doubt that a seat in council would have been his reward. As it was, he was sent from a place where he could do great good, to another where no one could do either good or harm—the Residency of Nagpore. In those days, it took at least a year to send despatches through the circumlocution offices of Calcutta to the India House, and the same period to get answers to them from the magnates there; but about two years after these events at Gwalior, Mr. Cavendish had the gratification of being informed that his official proceedings merited the highest approval of the Court of Directors—as they deserve, we think, the approbation of all right-minded people. The Court did more. Not to endanger the success of Mr. Cavendish's enlightened policy, the Directors ordered the immediate removal, of the Baiza Bye, and all her reactionary adherents, from Scindea's frontier.

Lest it should be thought by any one of the many admirers of the domestic policy in India of that excellent nobleman, Lord William Bentinck, that, in this little sketch of his foreign policy, we have given even the slightest touch of colouring, we will relate, by way of illustration, an amusing anecdote, which is known to three or four persons now living, and which sufficiently confirms our statement that, in respect of the rights of native states, his lordship entirely overlooked the tenth commandment. It happened that Major Sulterland was selected to fill the office vacated by Mr. Cavendish. He was at that period the most distinguished officer of 'Sillidar,' or irregular Horse, in India, as he was, later in life, the foremost man of his day in the diplomatic corps; but at that time he had had no experience as a Resident. He therefore waited on the Governor-General in Calcutta, to learn what the policy was to be at Gwalior;—was it to be intervention or non-intervention? Lord Bentinck, whose disposition, like that of Lord Palmerston, loved a joke, quickly replied: 'Look here, Major,' and his lordship threw back his head, opened wide his mouth, and placed his thumb and finger together like a boy about to swallow a sugar-plum. Then, turning to the astonished Major, he said: 'If the Gwalior State *will* fall down your throat, you are not to shut your mouth, as Mr. Cavendish did, but swallow it; that is *my* policy.' Rendered into plain words, this demonstrative instruction meant, 'If you find tumult in the capital, and general disorganisation on our frontier, whether occasioned by my permission to the Baiza Bye to carry on her intrigues, or otherwise, don't interfere by giving a young and inexperienced prince good and seasonable advice. We, as the paramount power, have, like Pecksniff, a "mission;" we can allow neither our own subjects on the border to be frightened, nor Scindea's own people to be oppressed; therefore, if it be our "mission" to suppress a badly-governed state, don't you stand in the way of it.' To 'the traditionary old Indians,' the objects of so much scorn in these days, this doctrine smacks of petty larceny. Imagine a magistrate of Bow Street to say to some smart-looking man, with a cloak hanging on his arm for a purpose, 'Don't prowl about the theatres at night, picking pockets, for that is larceny; but if you see a person drop his purse, keep it; a traditionary old beak would call this petty larceny, but I tell you it is all right!' In a moral point of view, we think the two cases exactly parallel. If we were alluding to Lord Bentinck's domestic policy, we should say, with unfeigned pleasure, that no Governor-General ever went to India who laboured more assiduously or more successfully than his lordship did, to improve the very low condition of the millions who, for six years, lived in the enjoyment of entire peace under his beneficent rule; and we transcribe, as evidence of his benevolence, the last paragraph of the last letter that he ever penned in India. It was addressed to the Begum Sumroo:—'To-morrow morning I embark for England; and my prayers and best wishes attend you, and all others who, like you, exert themselves for the benefit of the people of India.' Such noble words awaken the best sympathies of mankind.

The wheels of the government machine at Gwalior, which Mr. Cavendish had set in motion, continued their good course throughout the entire period of the young Rajah's reign; and all that need be added is, that, during the whole administration of Lord Auckland, which followed that of Lord Bentinck, no attempt was made to keep alive the old annexation-desire, nor were any overt acts done by the secretariat at Calcutta to pilfer the State of Gwalior.

Early in the year 1842, the people of England beheld, with sorrow and mourning, the result of the great fraudulent aggression which had been set in motion by the Whig ministry through the unwilling agency of that good but unfortunate man, Lord Auckland. We dethroned a popular and friendly monarch at Cabool, to put up a foolish and vile old pensioner, with a view to make him our convenient tool, to keep the Russians from sacking Delhi. We crave to be believed—to keep the Russians out of Delhi! This unrighteous, wretched, and silly policy of Sir John Cam Hobhouse, very greatly imperilled our empire in the East. Of an army and its followers at Cabool, not less in the aggregate than 20,000 men, the remnant reached Jellalabad on the wasted form of a starved and wounded pony. It was Dr. Brydon. With the exception of a few notables, kept by Uckbar Khan for his own especial interest, all, save the doctor, were first betrayed, and then butchered; the shivering Hindoo Sepoys being spared the sword that they might suffer a more lingering and cruel death by frost and hunger. The news of this frightful massacre reached our provinces in the month of February. It flew through the length and breadth of the land, and its awful sound rang in the ears of the natives of India. Never had such a disaster occurred to our arms since the day we first stepped from our ships on the swamps of Bengal. The English community in India felt that our prestige was gone, and 'whom shall we hang?' seemed to be the only enquiry. The thronged streets of the great Moslem cities teemed with 'the faithful,' whose bitter hatred of their Kaffir rulers was for a time broken by their utter astonishment. The 'Crescent' had signally replaced the 'Cross!' Providentially, the Hindoos sympathised with the Sepoys, their brethren and our fellow-sufferers, and there were then no greased cartridges or open tamperings with their religion to cause, as in 1857, the combination of the two races for the extinction of our power. But who, it was everywhere asked, is to appear and give something like reality to our strength, and restore our fortunes? We had no Reuter in those sad times; but suddenly there came into Calcutta from the steamer at the 'sand heads' a native runner with 'the express,' bringing the joyous tidings that Lord Ellenborough had arrived! For once—the fact is as we state it—for once the press of India was of one accord; and its accord was this, that Peel's selection of his Lordship was a most happy circumstance. All 'the people'—the people in India are the civil and military services, and the interlopers who abound in Calcutta;—the rest are the 'natives' of India;—all 'the people' were loud in their praise of his antecedents. He was the *protégé* of 'the Duke.' He had tamed, what Rarey in recent times has not attempted, a wild elephant. He had for years made India the subject of his studies, and having crammed himself with Munro, Elphinstone, and Malcolm, he would, it was said, shape his course after their beneficent manner. He had, too, in a sense, for some time past, governed India by 'controlling' the India House in Cannon Row. He was, likewise, a great debater in the Lords; and Calcutta folks, enamoured of Macaulay, who spoke with the greatest brilliancy in their town-hall, delight to have a first-class speaker; their out-going Governor, though if left to himself a most efficient administrator, being so deficient in the art of speaking, that he would not have been tolerated a second time in the penny depôt for orators at the north-east corner of Leicester Square. Who, then, 'the people' asked, could so well repair the edifice which had been well-nigh shattered to pieces by the Affghans as this most promising statesman?

He arrived in March, and began his career with the most astonishing success. Nott and Pollock gloriously led our troops to Cabool, rigorously punished our assailants, restored, and indeed greatly added to, our prestige, and brought back the captives in great triumph; Lord Ellenborough, seated on a magnificent elephant, proceeding to the left bank of the Sutledge to do homage to the victorious heroes.

But after this good beginning his Lordship's greatness abandoned him. He became the victim of a strange fanaticism—the fanaticism of self-admiration. We could name several great individuals who, like Lord Dundonald, have fallen the prey of malevolence; but we do not at this moment recollect any instance, in modern times, except this, of a very great reputation being suddenly wrecked by overweening vanity. In ancient history, we remember, it is recorded that Pompey never got over his conquest of Mithridates; but returning to Rome to obtain admiration, he was beset and ruined by that weakest of all failings, and his biographer tells us with much feeling that this hero was 'greatly pitied.' It was even so with his Lordship;—he was very much pitied. Looking back, at this distance of time, to the history of his career in India, we are at a loss to point to one redeeming act. His despatches promise no hope. In one of these he strangely pictured old Mahmoud of Guznee getting out of his tomb, where he had rested some centuries, and looking with surprise and indignation at General

Nott's sappers as they hurled the old gates of Sommauth from their rusty hinges. In another, ostentatiously dated 'The Pearl Mosque of the Taj,' he ludicrously addressed the male and female chieftains of India as his 'dear brothers and sisters.' We feel constrained to add, that Lord Ellenborough's sense of justice did not redeem him; for, with one stroke of his pen, without provocation and without notice, he removed from their very lucrative situations all the revenue and judicial officers in the Saugor and Nerbudda territories, vouchsafing this terse explanation that 'a new system required new men.' Suppose Mr. Gladstone, in another great effort this session, to bring in and pass a bill to repeal section this and caput that of the well-known statute of George the Second, and to permit publicans to water their brandies to any extent they pleased, would that novelty in the art of putting down intoxication, albeit 'a new system,' be any just reason for discharging Sir Thomas Fremantle, the able chairman of the excise, and the painstaking gentlemen who occupy all day the sombre chambers of Somerset House? No act of the many strange ones he committed drew down on his Lordship in India so much merited unpopularity as this most arbitrary proceeding. But in this, as in everything he did or wrote, we observe the Ellenborough individuality of character.

No one, however, will deny Lord Ellenborough the rare quality of the most perfect disinterestedness in the distribution of immense patronage. That he unfairly confined his richest gifts to one class of public servants, which was, we need hardly say, the military, thereby causing well-grounded jealousies among the civilians, is beyond all doubt true; but he freed himself altogether from the importunities of relations, the obligations of party, and the solicitations of his Secretaries; and it may be added, that he regarded no claim to the higher appointments as worthy of a moment's attention that was not based on approved military merit in the field; and it was in fact this one-sided disposition of the good things that fell into his hands that rendered his very name hateful among the civilians, and which, in the end, indirectly led to his downfall.

We come now to a period of great calamity to the House of Scindea; and if, in our relation of the public events, we appear, as we fear we shall, to be tedious, our excuse is, that the statement will be, on the whole, calculated to stagger credibility. We propose, with a view of being understood by readers who have not made the institutions of a native Court a matter of interest, to explain what is meant by a 'British Resident,' and 'The Durbar.' A 'Resident' is a man who has gained one of the richest prizes in the lottery of a public servant's career in India. He occupies, in or near the Capital of the native Princes, a splendid mansion, which was erected and furnished at the expense of the Supreme Government; receives a salary varying in amount, according to the importance of the State, from 5,000*l.* to 10,000*l.* a year, and, as the representative of the Governor-General himself, takes precedence at all ceremonials of everyone in the State, except the Maharajah. His duties are very light, and are similar to those performed by ambassadors in Europe. The most distinguished civilians and officers are selected for the office. Munro, Elphinstone, Ouchterlony, Malcolm, Metcalfe, Macnaghten, Cavendish, Sutherland, Sleeman, Hamilton, the two Lawrences, Mansel—indeed, nearly all the 'celebrities' of India—have been, at one time or other, 'Residents' at the foreign Courts. On accepting office they are instructed officially—which does not necessarily mean sincerely—to observe the strictest neutrality between conflicting interests in the Durbar; to avoid all interference in the internal management of the country; but are permitted to give friendly advice to the

Chief if he choose to ask for it, not otherwise. The Gwalior 'Durbar' is a Council of State, presided over by the Maharajah or, if he be a minor, by the Maharanee or Queen Mother, who sits on the throne concealed from public gaze by a curtain called a purdah. The members are the hereditary nobles of the State, the commandants of brigades, chiefly Christians of Portuguese and Italian extraction, and the leading men of the priesthood, who are of course Brahmins. The individual power and influence of the members differ according to the dignity of the office which they may happen to hold, and the greater number take no active part in public business, and attend only when summoned on formal occasions, such as royal birthdays, festivals, and military reviews; but the opinion of this body is regarded as the recognised opinion of the Principality, and its resolution makes and unmakes a minister, and, in very rare instances, as in the case of the Baiza Bye which we have detailed, deposes the regent if there happened to be a regency at the time; but—and the fact is important to remember—its acts are always considered as the direct acts of the Maharajah, or, during a minority, of the Queen Mother, even if, as at the period we are writing of, both were children of tender years,

In Gwalior, as in all other native Powers, the system of government is oligarchical. In the territories of Her Majesty the form is that of a mild despotism.

In this Durbar there were only three persons of capacity enough to occupy the post of minister. They were Bapoo Setolia, noted rather for being a man of the highest rank in the nobility than for business habits; Ram Rao Phalkea, who, when a young man, had commanded a Mahratta contingent under Lord Lake, and who, for his bravery and loyalty, enjoyed a large income from the British Government; and the Dada Khasjeewalla—he who had obtained for us the loan of a million when our treasury was empty—who, by virtue of the office of great Chamberlain and Keeper of the crown jewels, which was hereditary in his family, could command the influence, always very considerable, of the palace. It was in later times that this Gwalior Council produced a statesman whose equal had not been seen since our rule began—Dinker Rao; a man whom we have recently created a Maharajah, decorated with the 'star of India,' and placed in the legislative Council of Calcutta, on account of his pre-eminent abilities. Without these details we could hardly hope to make our narrative of an impending calamity intelligible to the reader.

On the 7th of February 1843, Maharajah Junkojee Scindea died suddenly, before he had made any arrangement for naming a successor; and as his widow was a mere child, only thirteen years of age, the right of election fell on the Durbar. It elected the nearest known male relative of the deceased Chief, Bhajeerutt Rao, a boy nine years old, who assumed thereupon the name of Gyajee Scindea. The great annexation-party in India, whenever there happened to be no direct heir to the throne of a native State, always set up a loud talk on the impolicy of allowing an adoption, but the British Government possessed no power to bar the act. As Sir Henry Lawrence rightly laid down the law and practice when he said, 'The confirmation of the Suzerain is necessary in all cases, but it does not appear that confirmation can be refused.' It is something like the fiction of the *congé d'élire* in respect of our bishops. In India, the sanction is a form that is very much prized, but the Governor-General—before the mutinies—was not the only Suzerain whose approval was sought. A messenger of high rank would be despatched with a nuzzur * to the Emperor of Delhi, who would send back in return a title. Thus, Junkojee Rao Scindea was created by the Emperor Junkojee Rao '*Alijah*'

* A large present of money.

Scindea; and that Mahommedan appellation of honour from the House of Timour was really much more highly valued than the mere formal confirmation by the Governor-General.

The next thing the Durbar had to do was to elect a minister, the Maharanee being the regent; and now the mischief began. As Lord Ellenborough had firmly resolved, though his resolution was not then made known, first to disregard the rights of this State, and afterwards to deprive it of its independence, the preliminary step would necessarily be to set aside the Maharanee on the ground of her infancy, and to put up in her place as Regent a person who would cheerfully do the bidding of the British Government. The election was in the hands of the Durbar. Now there was only one individual in that council who would lend himself to carry out an anti-national policy, and he was called the Mama-sahib. Accordingly, the Resident laid aside the principle of non-intervention which hitherto had guided his conduct, and strained every nerve to effect this man's election. We will give in this place a slight sketch of the candidate who was set up by us for the honours of the Regency. Of the meanest capacity and of low origin, he had been for many years the Potail of a hamlet in a remote part of the

Dekhan. In person he was so insignificantly small and slight, that, had he been born in Yorkshire, he would have found profitable employment in the stables of the North, and might possibly have ridden the winner of the St. Leger. He owed his seat in the Durbar to the lucky accident of a marriage, his pretty niece having been the first wife of Junkojee Scindea; and as she and her husband were at this period dead, he became, through the loss of these patrons, the butt and the object of pleasantry to the whole Council. His manners, too, like those of all upstarts, were repulsive; whilst his sole boast that he was the favourite at the Residency, which he undoubtedly was, inflamed the hatred that was everywhere else felt towards him. Excepting the troops which, with much forethought, he had himself inlisted, and which were always stationed round his house, it may be safely asserted that he had not an adherent in the Capital, and we think we may add, that he was the only man who exercised for three months the power and patronage of a Regency without the solace of a single sycophant. He had, it is true, been minister about the time of his niece's marriage, but he was conveniently released from the weight of governing, just as Mr. Addington was when Pitt and Fox were 'out,' by a power behind him. This, then, was the

Ellenborough candidate, and he was ably nominated by the British Resident. The opposition candidate, who, if there had been no interference, would have been elected by acclamation, was the Dada Khasjeewalla. Just at this critical time arrived a letter from his Lordship which conveyed these words:—'The Governor-General would *gladly* see the Regency conferred upon the Mama-sahib.' At this juncture news reached Gwalior that Sir Charles Napier had entered the city of Hydrabad, after two sanguinary battles, as a conqueror, and had made the Ameers, Chiefs of that State, prisoners of war. A proclamation, announcing the annexation of the country, followed. We offer no opinion of our own on that act of Lord Ellenborough's. Mr. Thornton, the historian, who had access to all the unpublished documents which were concealed from vulgar eyes in the recesses of the old India House, has characterised it as an affair of 'ambition, not philanthropy; cupidity, not benevolence;' declaring further, that 'it was sheer hypocrisy to declaim on the vices of the Ameers and the wrongs of their people, while, if our own interest had not furnished a spur to interference, the rulers might, for us, have revelled in their vices, and the people bent under their wrongs until the end of time.' (*Thornton*, vol. vi. p. 465.) Even Sir Charles Napier seemed to wince a little, though he acquired a great fortune by it, as he called the procedure, with his accustomed quaintness of expression, a 'humane bit of rascality.' We do not, we confess, detect much humanity in a matter which cost the lives of many thousands of our fellow-creatures: but he was not the first great general who knew how to mingle the deeds of the sword with the highest precept of the sacred book. However, all that concerns our narrative is to show that ominous clouds were seen in the political heavens, and it behoved the minor gods not to cross the path of the great son of Saturn. The Mama-sahib was, therefore, elected Regent, and the Resident placed on the throne the little Gyajee. The curtain fell on this first act of the drama.

As might have been foreseen, we think, a Regent on sufferance, without a party or public esteem or military support, was the mere caricature of a great officer, and one who could scarcely hope to meet with anything better from the Court or the people than contemptuous indifference. If nothing had been asked of him, on our requisition, his ordinary official business might possibly have been very tranquil; but it was hardly to be expected that, after the mere routine work was over, his great patrons would suffer him to repose all day on the soft cushions which form the Eastern throne. There happened to be, at this time, a little disturbance in a distant part of the country, between a party of villagers and some sepoys, and the Resident called on the Mama to cause the apprehension of the native officer who was in command of the men; but, unluckily, power to act was just the one thing which the Regent most wanted. He was helpless, and the temper of the Resident was chafed. What was, then, to be done? The latter addressed himself to Lord Ellenborough, and suggested the calling in of British troops from Agra. The answer seemed to make 'confusion worse confounded.' 'I intrust the use of troops to the discretion of no one except my own.' The pear was clearly not ripe, and nothing was done.

And now another and an awkward embarrassment appeared, which seemed to set the very teeth of the Regent as if he were in perfect terror. A slave-girl, whose name was Narungee, who had never been permitted to go outside the walls of the Zenana, had erected, it was gravely said, the standard of revolt in the palace. Let it not be thought that we are imposing on the reader's credulity, or attaching a higher importance to a supposed fact than at the first glance it might seem to warrant.

The name and alleged deeds of this simple girl actually formed topics for elaborate despatches, which may be read any day in the India House, in 'blue books,' and which are alluded to with absurd seriousness, in Thornton's great work on India. We, then residing on the spot, could never believe that she was anything better than the ordinary slave; but if we are to give entire credence to the affrighted Mama, she must have been a Gorgon in disguise. Her beautiful long hair must have been 'serpents,' and her teeth 'the tusk of a wild boar;' and, if she did not do what her immortal sisters did, 'turn her enemies into stones,' she did something almost as wonderful, for she deposed the nominee of the great Autocrat of India, packing him out of the country with all his baggage, without even the common Asiatic ceremony of the beat of a 'tom-tom.' We would not, if we could avoid it, add a particle of gall to the humiliation of this poor creature and his grand patrons, but a regard for truth compels us to add that, before taking his leave of Gwalior for ever, the ex-regent helped himself, out of the public treasury, to 40,000*l.* over and above the salary and perquisites of a three months' regency. Still, his humiliation must have far exceeded that of deposed monarchs of the West, for when he petitioned the Governor-General to restore him to power, the answer, it is said, crushed his spirit for life. 'You have proved yourself unfit,' said Lord Ellenborough, 'to manage either men or women, and a minister of Gwalior must manage both.' He proceeded to the hamlet in the Dekhan, and there resumed the humble office of Potail, his remaining days embittered by the recollection of a Governor-General's ingratitude. A guarantee was, however, vouchsafed to him against personal harm; for, as the India House historian informs us, 'the Resident was desired, if he entertained the least apprehension of danger to the Mamasahib, to address the Maharanee in the language of warning.' And what kind of warning was it to be? Mr. Thornton tells us. 'The threat was to be enforced by reference to the conduct recently adopted by the British Government to the Ameers of Scinde.' (*Thornton*, vol. vi. p. 476.) That conduct had become, it was now clear, the formula—not of the British Government we are quite certain—but of the Governor-General, and it was very much harsher than any that had ever before been put into practice since we governed the country.

Before we proceed any further with our narrative, we will turn over a few leaves of 'Thornton,' to see what he, the mouthpiece—if we may use the word without offence—of the great East India Company, says on this signal failure of possessing 'influence' within the Durbar, whereby certain ulterior purposes, it was expected, would be peaceably carried into effect; but we will not be diverted into the consideration, at present, of what those purposes might be, as they were not exactly defined, we are certain, at this period, in the Governor-General's own mind. We confess, indeed, that we are inclined to regard the ejection of the Mama-sahib as a very great blunder, as it gave a fresh motive to Lord Ellenborough to mature some other scheme, which, as we shall see, proved far more certain to cause the collapse of the independence of this State, than the worst acts of a wretched imbecile could possibly bring about. We believe, in fact, that if Lord Ellenborough did not actually rejoice over the expulsion of his nominee, which the insulting reply to the man's appeal would alone justify us in thinking, still, perceiving that from him nothing great could be derived, the only umbrage which he felt, perhaps, was the apparent contempt done to his dignity, which the overthrow of his favourite would seem to display. But we will see what Mr. Thornton says on the subject. 'The facility with which the surrender of the Dada Khasjeewalla ('an incident which we have yet to relate) had been yielded under the influence of terror, imposed by the march of the British force, seems to have effected a change in the policy of the Governor-General, and he determined to employ that TERROR as an instrument for obtaining those ulterior objects which, less than two months before he had been content to leave to the effect of influence. . . . . Thus,' proceeds the historian, 'what was on the 1st of November (the date of a secret minute, not of the policy) proposed to be left to "influence," was on the 20th of December TO BE EXTORTED AT THE POINT OF THE BAYONET. . . . . He fairly throws over the Mama.' What do we read in the public press of London at this present day? 'Any attempt at encroachment on the sovereignty of the Danish crown by the German powers, would bring to Denmark not merely barren sympathy, but the powerful assistance of those who have the means of preventing a small but independent and well-regulated state from being crushed by a great confederacy.' Happy Denmark! but whose powerful assistance could be invoked by the youthful Maharanee?

We return to our narration. It was on the 24th of May 1843, that the Mama took flight; and on the 26th, the Maharanee, who now occupied the throne as Regent, ordered the Durbar to assemble to elect a Minister. This national council made choice at once of the Dada Khasjeewalla. Vacillation of purpose was one of the remarkable traits in the character of the Governor-General, and an instance of it was to be given now. He who had refused to recognise the Maharanee in February on account of her tender years, hesitated not to acknowledge her as Regent in May; but no power under heaven would have prevailed on him to countenance, as Minister, the ill-fated Chamberlain. A wit, whose name we cannot remember, once said, that—

> Women's faults are two—
> Nothing's right they say, nothing right they do.

It was so with this man. The same number of faults, though in their character different, had all the native Chiefs in India, whenever their respective territories chanced to be coveted. They had, it was alleged, in stereotyped letter-press, a weak system of government on the frontier, and a strong system of government in the interior. 'The wrongs of the people,' which foreshadowed the seizure of Scinde, illustrate 'the strong system.' The unbridled freedom of the people means, in Indian diplomacy, 'the weak system,' and that was now to be advanced on the accession of the odious Minister of Gwalior. 'It is a matter,' writes the Governor-General, 'of paramount importance that there should exist in Gwalior a government willing and able to preserve tranquillity along that extended line (meaning the frontier), for the British Government cannot permit the growing up of a lax system of rule, generating habits of plunder along its frontier.' (*Thornton*, p. 472.) When this is written in despatches, the evidence of approaching danger is strong and undissembled; but what will the reader think when we tell him that the province of Bundlekhund, which was under our control, and the two rich provinces of Saugor and the Nerbudda, which were absolutely British territory (the frontiers of which bordered on the frontiers of Scindea's dominions), were at this time, and had been for two years, in a state of open insurrection; and that on the very day that this threatening despatch was penned by Lord Ellenborough, Scindea's Contingent of 2,000 men were keeping our rebels from destroying the wealthy town of Khimlassa, which was distant 100 miles from the Gwalior Capital, and which belonged to the British Government, whilst the most active and able officer of the Maharanee's army, Colonel Salvadore, with his men, was saving from destruction Balabehut, another town of ours, which the rebels were about to fire. It was thought that the great heat of the season would be perilous to British soldiers, so those of the Maharanee had been borrowed. This was no border disturbance, but a most extensive and marked demonstration against our power, which had commenced as soon as our troops left India for Cabool, and it was to aid in the suppression of this rebellion that our friendly ally, Scindea, was lending his troops. At the least, fifty villages in these three districts were laid waste, the inhabitants flying to the jungles. A Civilian riding through the country was shot dead by a concealed matchlock-man. An Officer, marching at the head of his company through the narrow pass of Narhut, was 'picked off' by an unseen rebel. A servant of an English officer accidentally falling, or voluntarily getting down from the howdah of his master's elephant, was seized and his head instantly cut off and carried away as a trophy, almost within reach of the animal, and in sight of his employer! Was this a rather 'lax system of government,' we wonder? It may cause a passing smile if we record the fact that a ringleader of this small rebellion, on being brought before Colonel Sleeman, who had the controlling of these three provinces, was asked by the great functionary why he, whose landed possessions had been lightly assessed, could possibly want those of his neighbour. The man drew himself up at full length, looked hard at the Colonel, and replied that his conduct was not particularly singular, for he knew people who, when they held all Hindoostan, on no assessment whatever, must need go as far as Affghanistan in search of a little more! This strain of irony was, in its way, almost as good as that indulged in by St. Paul when he was questioned by Ananias, but we dare not pursue the comparison.

We pass on to the next aspect of affairs, since nothing came from 'the influence' within the Durbar, or from the ungenerous threat of having, as alleged, 'a lax system on the frontier.' This was how to get the Resident out of the country, and yet 'lull all suspicion' (*Thornton*): a very ingenious problem. We are now in the height of the rain season; and it was necessary at once, if ever, that matters should be 'coming up'—if we may use the expressive language of a Thames waterman—'on the top of a flood-tide.' The Governor-General thus addressed the Resident:—'The great heats usually lead you at this season to absent yourself from Gwalior, and I see no sufficient reason for your now departing from your usual course.' The idea was not bad in itself, if such a very small game was worthy a great Governor-General to play; but the fact was just the other way. The Resident was a fine, handsome, strong man, who cared no more for 'great heats' than a salamander does; and, as he had a very large family, it was anything rather than agreeable for him to leave the spacious mansion of the Residency for a small Maida-hill-like villa on the right bank of the Chumbul, which the Rajah of Dholpoor kept for the use of English dâk travellers. The Resident felt that he *must* acquiesce, as it would not be safe to disregard a hint which so considerately concerned his bodily comfort. He accordingly told the Durbar a little fib, and this was that he required 'change of air.' We give the Resident's own explanation, just as he wrote it to Lord Ellenborough:—'The Maharanee's vaqueel replied that this was not the season at which I usually moved. I said no; but that as I had nothing particular to engage my attention at present, I should go to Dholpoor.' The vaqueel still pressing his objection, 'I requested him to inform the Maharanee that she was aware that I was in the habit of moving about occasionally, and that she must look upon my going to Dholpoor, on this occasion, as nothing more than that I had stated, and that she must not think that I was offended with her that I went there.' (*Thornton.*) Let not the reader for a moment imagine that because Colonel Spiers felt himself bound to yield to the Governor-General's suggestion, that he was capable of deception towards the young princess. Nothing had *then* transpired to lead him to apprehend a storm; nothing to show very clearly duplicity; nothing to raise the fear of another 'humane bit of rascality.' He had, as a public servant, obligations to fulfil, but, even if a little weak as we fear that he was, he was a man of the highest honour, and meant all that he said when he gave this assurance to the Maharanee 'that he was not offended with her.' Well, in the middle of the monsoon, the country everywhere flooded, the Resident, the assistant-Resident, the clerks, the native doctor, camels, horses, cows, sheep, goats, and all the various inhabitants of the poultry-yard, sped, as well as they could through water and mud, to the turbid stream of the Chumbul, to avoid 'the great heats,' said Lord Ellenborough; 'for change of air,' avowed the Resident; 'to lull suspicion,' writes Mr. Thornton! All that we know is that a more complete exodus had not taken place at the Residency in our time. Not a thirsty sparrow was to be seen on the housetops.

The problem, which we described as ingenious, was now to be solved, or, perhaps, we may be permitted to say, that the sensation scene of the drama was now to be placed on the stage by the great

Boucicault of India. Without a word of warning, or of explanation of 'the reason why,' the Resident and the assistant-Resident,* who were scarcely settled down in the Rajah's villa, received notice that they were dismissed from their respective appointments, —doomed never to behold again their dearly-loved Gwalior! No idea of the universal astonishment can be conjectured. A perfect multitude of guesses was made, and rumours of every kind were spread through the Gwalior Capital. The great question was whether the dismissal was a matter for exultation to the Court, or an indication of the coming death-blow to the independence of the State. All doubts on those points were soon set at rest when it was seen that Colonel Sleeman had been appointed the new Resident. An able and a distinguished diplomatist,—a philanthropist, also, if princes and nobles did not unfortunately form a portion of mankind—he was known, though he had never been a week, during a long career in India, within the Gwalior territory, to hold the most violent opinions against the House of Scindea, and had, before his appointment was made, sent to England a work to be published, in which his deliberate opinions were thus recorded:— 'As a citizen of the world I could not help thinking that it would have been a great blessing upon a large portion of our species if an earthquake were to swallow up this Court of Gwalior and the army that surrounds it.' Mr. Thornton, remarking on this subject, tells us that it did not appear very clear, from any papers in the India House, why Colonel Spiers was dismissed; but, possibly, the transcript, which we have made from a work which six months afterwards was circulated all over India, may give some clue to the mystery.

A crime of a very black description indeed was now to be advanced against the Dada Khasjeewalla, the supplanter of Lord Ellenborough's nominee. It was said—by whom we do not know—by either Colonel Spiers or Colonel Sleeman—and readily enough believed by Lord Ellenborough, that the Minister of the State had intercepted a letter from his lordship to his dear young 'sister,' the Maharanee. Now, what really occurs in the zenana of an oriental palace must always be a matter of great doubt to European functionaries; but we waive that consideration altogether, accept the charge as proved, and convict the minister of —— what? 'A high crime against the Maharanee,' declared the Governor-General. The letter was written in the Persian language, and the Maharanee, a child of thirteen, could neither read nor write any language at all. There was only one man in the Capital who, by virtue of his hereditary office of 'Great Chamberlain and Keeper of the crown jewels,' could enter the most sacred of the female apartments, and that man was the Dada Khasjeewalla. The word *Khasjeewalla* means 'Keeper of the jewels,' it being from this office that he derived his name. No matter who was minister, there was his place whenever he pleased to go to it. Who then, except this man, had the privilege to open and read the Governor-General's letter, to say nothing of his right as the chosen minister of the nation? To suppose that this man, the favourite of the palace, cared to keep in ignorance a child, not out of the nursery, of the contents of a letter, albeit they conveyed censures upon himself, is in the last degree Quixotic. The only thing that can be said to explain the whole affair is '*delenda est Carthago*;' and, that being so, that this charge, contemptible as we regard it, would do as well as any other.

Some very clever writers in England say, however, 'that nothing is more ludicrous than the application of western principles to oriental affairs.' We think that if the western principles be good, they will do as well for the east as the west,—for the black as for the white man. If the French, now that Greece has not a king, were to seize that classic land, 'the western principles' would be paraded to show that the act was an outrage; but when Scinde was taken to enable our steamers to pass up the Indus, it was said to be laughable to apply 'western notions.' Or suppose that Count Ratazzi intercepted a letter from Louis Napoleon to his 'cousin' Victor Emanuel. What then? Recall the French ambassador? Let us see what Lord Ellenborough did. He peremptorily demanded that the Court of Gwalior should make over *to him* this daring Dada for punishment, though what the punishment was which his lordship intended he did not deign to say. We need hardly remark that such a demand struck at the very honour of the Raj, and that compliance with it would have covered the State, in the eyes of all the princes of India, with unutterable scorn and derision. The Durbar met and consulted, and, in the Maharanee's name, did everything to appease Lord Ellenborough's wrath. It instantly removed the Minister and placed him in confinement, putting in office Ram Rao Phalkea, whose loyalty to the British Government had been proved when he fought for us by the side of Lord Lake. It then, in the most submissive terms, declared its inability to deliver him up. Its *izzut*—a peculiarly expressive word signifying all that they hold dear—prevented it. Any punishment which his lordship would order, it was ready to inflict. But Lord Ellenborough was inexorable, and the nobles were apparently firm. The Governor-General now assembled one army on the north and another on the east frontier of Scindea's dominions, with the intention to be ready for an invasion *if the Dada Khasjeewalla were not given up.* It should be remembered that six months only had elapsed since the Ameers of Scinde were sent as prisoners of war to Calcutta; and three months only since Lord Ellenborough had, with singular good taste, threatened to treat the Chiefs of Gwalior 'after the same manner.' Their fears or their love of country prevailed, and they sent the Dada a prisoner to Agra, where the Governor-General was daily expected to join, and, as some foolish people imagined, to command the army of the north. There was, then, 'his pound of flesh,' and those who ever saw the obese Brahmin will not doubt that his lordship had a very good pound too. By order of Lord Ellenborough this alleged intercepter of a letter was BANISHED FOR LIFE, thereby necessarily losing the great emoluments of a hereditary office of high dignity. Ten years afterwards he died in exile, of dropsy, the effect of long-continued grief, in the holy city of Benares. It may be recollected that when Sir Robert Peel sent his lordship to India, he had for his Home Secretary of State Sir James Graham. About the same period when the Dada intercepted, as it was said he did, a letter to a child who could not read, and whose minister he was, the Home Secretary intercepted the letter of an Italian patriot, who foolishly relied on the supposed inviolability of the English post-office. The coincidence, no doubt, struck the mind of the Governor-General. One was banished for life, while the other, the Cumberland baronet, continued to 'eat pleasant bread, and fill his mouth with flesh and wine,' as unconcernedly as ever, at the cabinet dinners of Lord Ellenborough's patron. This illustrates, as well as anything we know, the natural love of equal justice among us.

Whenever a Chief, or the minister of a Chief, has the misfortune to come under the ban of a Governor-General it is extraordinary what a monster he is all at once represented to be. The following astonishing allegations were advanced, for the first time, in 1843, though the atrocity itself, to which they point, occurred, if indeed it did take place, in 1836. That the writer of the story gave ònly a *bonâ fide* expression of his belief, we do not for a moment doubt; but it proceeded from one who had had no knowledge of the Court or of the Minister, while the tale itself had never been heard before by anyone who had resided many years at Gwalior. That it was implicitly credited by the Governor-General may be assumed by the fact, that he remitted the statement to the Court of Directors; and it found a final resting-place in the pages of a great history, though it was not deemed necessary either to charge the man with the crime or to ascertain if there were the slightest foundation in respect of it. We should not have made any allusion to this native fabrication were it not to amuse the reader with an account of the manner by which the birth of a daughter, in a royal zenana, may, with the smallest amount of good luck, which, however, was absent on this occasion, be metamorphosed into that of a son and heir. The device is new to us, and appears a very ingenious one. A number of married women—interesting married women perhaps we should say—was introduced into the palace, and placed in a row on beds, like the inmates of a chamber of a lying-in hospital. Around the women were midwives, sorcerers, charmers, and, we imagine, the Khasjee himself—the poor husband knowing nothing and seeing nothing. But we will give the *official* tale. 'I may here be permitted,' wrote the Resident to Lord Ellenborough, 'to mention something of the character of the usurping minister.' We do not quite perceive why a man who was elected to his office as minister, precisely as Lord Ellenborough's nominee, the Mama, was, should be designated as a usurper. He was rather, we think, the unlucky supplanter of a wretched imbecile, and became very odious in certain influential quarters in consequence; but we pass on to the tale. 'He is considered to be, personally, a great coward, and to owe all his influence to intrigues. When the wife of the late Chief, Junkojee, was to be confined, he, the Khasjee, collected several women who expected to be confined about the same time, with a view to substitute a boy, should the Maharanee give birth to a girl. She gave birth to a daughter, but the birth of a son was announced by the Resident to the Supreme Government, and royal salutes were fired on the occasion. The fact of the child being a daughter was concealed from Scindea himself for ten days, till all the other women had given birth to daughters, and the Khasjee had no longer any hope of being able to substitute a boy. Scindea, as soon as he became acquainted with the truth, sent to the Resident, and, with unfeigned sorrow and mortification, made the falsehood known to him.' We do not pretend to be acquainted with anything which occurs within the zenana, but what we do know is, that on the 5th of April the Resident was informed that the Maharanee had given birth to a son, and that on the 7th, or two days later, it was stated that some mistake had occurred, and that the child was a daughter. We were present when the Maharajah's vaqueel explained, as well as he could, the error that had been made, or the deceit which had been practised, and we can produce a journal, whenever it is required, in which the following entries may be seen in it—'5th April. An heir to the House of Scindea was born this day.—7th April. The heir turns out to be an heiress!' The narrative proceeds to tell us, that 'it is *generally* believed that the Khasjee intended to poison, or otherwise destroy, the father, could he have succeeded in substituting the boy; and he is known to have employed all kinds of supposed sorcerers and charms to make away with him, in the hope that the Supreme Government would, as in the case of the Baiza Bye, allow his widow to adopt a son, which would secure him a long minority. The mother and daughter both died, and Scindea married the Tara Bye, a girl now thirteen years of age, who was permitted to adopt a boy, who is now about nine years old.' Such is the story. To us, on the very face of it, it seems perfectly incredible, and we presume to insist on this, as a matter of fairness, that the Governor-General was bound to have ordered some little investigation into this heavy charge before he consigned the man to perpetual exile.

The Dada having been given up, there was then an end of the *casus belli.* Nothing of the kind. 'I have found,' said his Lordship to the new Minister, Ram Rao Phalkea, who had been sent by the Durbar to Agra to wait on him, 'a clause in a treaty made with Dowlut Rao Scindea at Boorhanpoor, which obliges the British Government, if at any time Scindea should be unable to cope with his enemies, to afford him military assistance. It is true, indeed, that the clause carefully guards against the danger of a great military power forcing its unsolicited assistance on a very weak one by the insertion of the words "*on the requisition of the Maharajah*;" but it is impossible, on account of his tender years, for Gyajee Scindea to make the requisition, and, as I am the only judge of his necessities, I shall march my army to Gwalior.' The genius of Æsop never put into the mouth of a wolf stronger reasoning than this. Ram Rao Phalkea, who related this to us, was astounded, as well he might be, and replied—his hands joined as in the way of humble entreaty—that 'as nothing whatever had been mooted on the Boorhanpoor treaty, he had brought with him no copy of it to refer to; that it was notorious that it had been entered into by Dowlut Rao solely to enable him to put down the Pindarees' (the land-pirates who swarmed at that period in Central India); 'and that the invasion of a friendly state on such a pretext was quite a strange anomaly in the conduct of the Honourable Company.' And he was perfectly correct. But all argument, all protestations failed, as would those of a goose who, with equal pertinacity, declined the proffered aid of a hungry fox. So the armies advanced and crossed the frontier, and the battles of Maharajpoor and Punniar were the result. We of course gained two easy victories, and we lost one General and rather more than 1,000 men. The Mahrattas, called in the despatches 'our enemy,' lost, in round numbers, 5,000. The Maharanee, all the members of the Durbar, and all the officers of Scindea's army except two, knowing the utter hopelessness of success, and fearing the consequences of opposition, remained in their houses. The two exceptions were Major John Jacob and Major Alexander. Both were born at Gwalior, neither had attained the age of twenty-five, and both held a very lucrative command under this as well as under the former Maharajah. They were Christians, and had received an English education. For their audacity in having, from a sense of honour, led their respective brigades into action, they, like the Dada Khasjee-walla, were BANISHED FOR LIFE. We never heard what ultimately became of Major Alexander, but the fate of poor Jacob was a very sad one. A great chess-player, as most orientals are, he became at Agra a favourite of the Civilians and Officers who resided there. On the breaking out of the mutiny of 1857 the English were compelled to leave their houses to find safety in the fortress, and Jacob was invited to follow their example. Believing that the hostility of the rebels was directed against the people of England only, and relying on the popularity which attached to him among the natives as an exile, he remained in his house which was in the middle of the city. The cupidity of a servant led the wretch to murder his master, but his family, who were of course Christians, were unmolested—a proof that the cry of 'our religion in danger' was a mere pretence, and that the slaughter of our poor women and children arose, not from the fact that they were Christians, but that they were related to a Government which, with all its good intentions and good works, was not loved by the army or the upper classes of India.

The day before a shot was fired, Lord Ellenborough issued a proclamation in the English language, intended, we presume, for the people of England, in which he explained his intentions. In it we find that his Lordship was much moved by sentiments of pity towards the Maharajah; by a determination to brook no hostility to the British Government by *individuals* at his Court; and by a desire to have—which is the old story when the appetite for a native State is particularly sharp—*a quiet frontier.* This remarkable State document had more than one weak point in it. The date of the proclamation was the 19th of December. On the 1st of November, in a secret Minute, which Mr. Thornton has had the unkindness to give to the world, Lord Ellenborough lets out the secret why he meant to go to Gwalior to disband Scindea's army. Instead of Thornton and Ellenborough, the reader will think that he has Alison and Napoleon before him. 'To maintain unimpaired the position we now hold is a duty, not to ourselves alone, but to *humanity.*' We stop here to observe, that four great battles were fought this year, not to gratify ambition, still less to gain the coronet of an earl, but out of very tenderness to the human race! 'The adoption of new views of policy, weakness under the name of moderation, and pusillanimity under that of forbearance, would not avert from our own subjects, and from our own territories, the evils we let loose upon India; and the only result of false measures would be to remove the scene of a contest, altogether inevitable, from Gwalior to Allahabad, there to be carried on with diminished force, a disheartened army, and a disaffected people.' What is meant by this most extraordinary language? If a contest were altogether inevitable, why should it be at Allahabad? why with a diminished force? why with a disheartened army? why with a disaffected people? Excepting the little rebellion in Bundlekhund, carried on by a horde of matchlockmen without a gun, if loyalty and contentment did not pervade the whole length and breadth of our empire in India, passive obedience most certainly did. Then what could be meant? Well, we will unravel the mystery. It was all owing to a Napoleonic instinct! It was surmised, that the recent demise of Runjeet Sing would lead to struggles for the masterdom of the Punjaub; that a proud army at Lahore might even venture to cross the Sutledge and try its mettle against British soldiers; and that it was just possible that we might have to fall back upon Allahabad. There we should find the Gwalior army ready to kick us nearer to Calcutta, and it was clear that, under this marvellous change of fortune, our force would be 'diminished,' our army 'disheartened,' and the people 'disaffected.' So then, 'pity towards Gyajee Scindea;' the determination to brook no hostility by 'individuals at his Court' (that is, by the Dada Khasjeewalla and the Gorgon); and the desire to have 'a quiet frontier,' were what the lawyers call false colourings and pretences, the real motive being Napoleonic strategy, which taught Lord Ellenborough to destroy even an unoffending army rather than allow it to exist in his rear. His Lordship told us something amusing, it will be recollected, about the spectre of poor old Mahmoud of Guznee being suddenly roused from his tomb by General Nott's sappers. We wonder if it occurred to Lord Ellenborough to imagine the indignation of the ghosts of Vattel and Grotius when they 'looked down' on his Lordship at Gwalior.

Respecting the clause in the Boorhanpoor treaty on which the Governor-General pretended to justify the invasion, it cannot be controverted that there was no such treaty in existence. That which had been made in 1804, containing a stipulation of the kind alleged, was signed to meet the difficulties arising from the inroads of the Pindarees, but abrogated the following year to serve our own interests.

The whole thing was a barefaced sham, and was, as Mr. Thornton well described it, owing to 'the facility with which the surrender of the Dada had been yielded, under the influence of TERROR imposed by the march of the British force, that a change in the policy of the Governor-General was effected, and the determination arrived at to employ that TERROR as an instrument for obtaining ulterior objects.'

Much political capital was made out of the commotion which sprung up in the Capital soon after the dismissal of Colonel Spiers and his zealous assistant, Captain Ellis, from the Residency. It was said, and with some truth, that the army was disorganised. But what else was to be expected when every British officer in the neighbourhood was giving utterance to expressions, which were known to be only too true, that the Gwalior army was to be immediately disbanded? What would have occurred in our own empire if a notification had been made that our great Sepoy force was to be broken up? It was even stated authoritatively, in demi-official and private letters, what the arrangements, even to the minutest details, were to be. Twenty thousand men, it was said, were to be paid their wages and banished from their homes, and yet were expected to maintain their wonted attitude of military obedience.

Not a single act of hostility was committed against the Maharanee, whose popularity could not be gainsaid; nor one against the nobles, until the fact became known that they feared to stand up for the cause of their Sepoys. Some of the Officers, indeed, requested their men to place them in confinement, as a device, lest the displeasure of the British Government should be visited on them if they seemed to be free agents. Some apprehended the confiscation of their property. This was particularly the case in respect of their General-in-Chief, Jean Baptiste, who got himself locked up by his men because he had 40,000*l*. in 'Company's paper;' yet all this was complained of as the clearest proof of the overbearing insolence of the Mahratta Sepoys. They were angry and noisy enough, and they greatly distrusted their Christian officers, and some menaced them; but there was nothing in their behaviour that implied either disrespect to their own Government or hostility to ours.

Of the battles we presume to say very little, and that will not be in very high commendation. At Maharajpoor, the position even of the enemy was not known until a half-spent ball, bounding under an elephant which was carrying some officer of rank, or a lady who accompanied our forces, arrested attention. The army was not drawn up in order of battle, after the manner of Napier, but the men, bravely lead by their Officers, rushed to their work like lions let loose. Lord Ellenborough, mounted on his war-horse, was seen wherever danger was greatest, urging on the troops like a Marquis of Anglesea! His personal daring seemed to have had complete mastery over every consideration, especially over the least honoured of the seven cardinal virtues which we call prudence. Let us imagine that a stray shot had killed the great Governor of India. Ten millions of Mahommedans would have declared and believed that the hand of Divine wrath had guided the bullet for his Lordship's outrageous insult to their religion in the recent matter of the Somnauth gates; and the Mahratta sepoys would have sung songs of triumph to the day of their death. Even a general rising might have occurred. One atrocity, which was very horrible, was done by a small party of our soldiers. Some Mahratta sepoys, twenty or thirty in number, having discharged their last cartridge, were fleeing from the field, but, finding themselves surrounded by our troops, they rushed into a native's house, the family having fortunately abandoned it, and barricaded the doors. Some of our men, in a state of temporary frenzy let us hope, set fire to the thatched roof, and these miserable sepoys were burnt to ashes. As long as a month afterwards the walls of the house and the charred remains of the men could be seen by any traveller just as they had been left on the day of the battle—deliberately allowed to remain by an angry people with a view to cause a feeling of deeper hatred than ever against our race. At the intercession of an European officer, a personal friend of Ram Rao Phalkea the minister, the walls were taken down, the remains removed, and the soil ploughed for cultivation, to prevent the spot from being visited as the place of martyrs.

At Punniar, the battle, such as it was, was fought and won under the command of a very skilful and brave young officer of the Engineers, Alexander Cunningham, aide-de-camp to General Grey, whose severe indisposition confined him at the time to his tent. An act of almost greater atrocity, because done in cold blood, occurred here. A young Portuguese officer, as soon as his regiment had been dispersed, went up, on the field, to one of our brigade-majors, and, presenting his sword, asked to have his life spared. The brigade-major, a man of undoubted honour and feeling, declined the sword, and expressed his willingness to do all he could, and desired him, with much earnestness, to keep close by his side. Unhappily, the Major was on horseback, while the Portuguese was on foot. A demon in the rear had kept his tigerish eyes on the poor fellow, and a chance occurring, he plunged a bayonet through his body, making an exclamation while doing so in language too frightful to repeat. It may be added that Scindea's Contingent was, with exquisite taste, made to act against that State of whose salt the Officers and men of that body had long partaken, some of the latter being of the same village and country from which Gyajee Scindea had recently come. Happy is it for the vast masses which constitute the population of our empire that their Government is now carried on in the name of Her gracious Majesty, and that that which redounds to *her* honour and dignity, and to the good of both princes and people, can alone guide the acts of her viceroys for the future, and not their ambition and vanity.

There was a curious character in a story related in 'Blackwood' which we read many years ago. His name, if we recollect rightly, was Job Pippins. He was a man who made it the great rule of his life to feel his way. Well, after the flush of two easy but costly victories had passed off, Lord Ellenborough began to perceive the necessity of feeling *his* way.

His army had fought two battles in February 1843 to get to Hydrabad. It had contended in two places, Maharajpoor and Punniar, in December 1843 to reach Gwalior. He had seized Scind; could he, now that the recent conflicts had somewhat changed the aspect of affairs, annex Scindea's dominions? Consistency and our rapaciousness for territory urged him to take; the promise of 'assistance' and the expressions of 'pity' would make the taking look very awkward. Sir Herbert Maddock, it was understood, was consulted. He was at the time second to his Lordship in dignity, and vice-president of the council of Calcutta. He was for annexation. Colonel Sleeman, whose opinions, after a very short experience, had entirely veered round, and who no longer wished that 'an earthquake should swallow up the Court,' was unceasingly urging extreme moderation. The Resident went even so far as to consult Sir Herbert whether he ought not to resign. Then the country was richer than Scinde, and had been long coveted, as we have shown, by the great party of annexationists; but what most deprived these considerations of all force were the debates in Parliament. Mail after mail from England conveyed a whole load of invective on his Lordship's extravagant proceedings. The railings, too, came from men of mark in the

House. Vernon Smith, who had long been looked upon by his party as the fittest man to 'control' unruly Governor-Generals, and who had his eyes directed wistfully to Cannon Row, declared his belief that 'Lord Ellenborough's head was quite turned, and that he ought not to hold an appointment which invested him with the uncontrolled dominion of a great empire.' Sir Robert Inglis, though a high tory, was indignant, and his anger was only in a degree subdued by Sir Robert Peel assuring the honourable baronet that his Lordship 'had returned thanks to Almighty God in 1842 for the restoration of PEACE!' Lord John was unpardonably personal, declaring that 'Lord Ellenborough was not a man in whose hands such an empire as that of India could safely be left,' and added, 'that his Lordship would relieve this country from a great difficulty, and India from a great peril, if he retired.' No doubt that this stir in the House spoke to the mind—if we may use the term — of the Governor-General. The idea of annexation, at all events, was now abandoned, and a flaming notification went forth, 'announcing, as the result of the battles which had been fought—' what does the reader imagine?—the secure establishment in his independence of our little hero, Gyajee Scindea, on whose account this little sketch of his House has been written? Nothing of that kind—'the secure establishment of *British supremacy*!' (*Thornton*, vol. vi. chap. vi.) The same historian tells us, on the best possible authority, that 'the issue of his Lordship's official papers appeared to have had no other purpose, but to give expression to a feeling of triumph, and to gratify a desire of treating the Gwalior State as a conquered country. . . . . . Judging from the language held on the subject, it seems to have been thought an act of *extraordinary lenity that the State should have been suffered to exist at all*!'

Before we entirely leave this strange developement of a procedure which began by an undignified act of meddling in the election of a Minister, and ended by humbling in the dust the steadiest ally which the British Government then possessed in India, we ought, as a matter of justice, to tell aloud who the persons were that rescued this State from annexation. We are perfectly certain, though the fact does not admit of positive proof, that it was the fear of rousing once more the resentment of powerful individuals in Parliament that just turned the scale and no more in favour of Scindea. In fact, hardly an attempt was made at one time to conceal the intention to annex; the only real obstacles that stood in the way of the act were the hereditary rights of the Maharajah. It was impossible, by any conceivable sophistry, to make little Gyajee Scindea, at his age, appear as a political delinquent; but it was a comparatively easy task to hold up his pretensions as being in themselves contemptible, and thereby remove all fear of his having, in the event of his downfall, any-one's sympathy in *England*. It was, we believe, with that view that Lord Ellenborough described the boy, in a secret Minute, 'as a relative of robber-chiefs,' and as one 'who was elected by the zenana and the chiefs of the army for their sole benefit, not for that of *the people*.' The allusion to 'the people' was such a telling expedient—such a beautiful means to an end—coming, too, as it did from the pen of a friend of extreme democracy! But if those opinions were honestly entertained, why were they not openly expressed in February, when Lord Ellenborough publicly recognised the child as the proper heir to the throne? An overstrained delicacy was surely not the reason, as that feeling did not very often oppress his mind at any time. It was the opportune and vehement invective of Lord John Russell, Mr. Vernon Smith, Sir Robert Inglis, and others, that really saved this prince, and, as we shall show when we come to the period of the great mutiny, rescued, through the instrumentality of this 'relation of robbers,' the cause of our empire from becoming, at a critical time, absolutely desperate. If, as Sir John Lawrence truly remarked, 'a succession of miracles saved us,' one of the miracles was most assuredly our having, in the darkest hour of our peril, an unflinching, a thoughtful, and a brave friend in Maharajah Gyajee Scindea. 'The Star of India,' which Her Majesty conferred on him, sets all question of the character of his services beyond disputation.

Gwalior stands midway between Maharajpoor and Punniar. To ensure the greatest amount of pomp, Lord Ellenborough ordered his imperial tent to be pitched on the great plains of Bamor, distant four miles from the Capital, and then issued directions to both his armies to unite and take up a position around him. The tragedy being over, it was a great relief to everyone's mind to learn that the next thing to be seen was a kind of 'extravaganza.' Susceptible of profound ridicule as all that followed most undoubtedly was, we intend to relate the transactions in terms of the most perfect sobriety. The Governor-General had resolved, not only to have a victory, but to enjoy a triumph. Accordingly, he desired that the Maharajah and the members of the Durbar should wait on him in his gaudy tent, surrounded as it was by the finest and best disciplined army that had been seen in Scindea's dominions since the period of Ranojee Scindea, the slipper-bearer. They were to appear, not to hear, indeed, that their country was seized, but to yield their independence for ever. Gyajee Scindea, being only in his ninth year, had to be thoroughly schooled by the master of the ceremonies within the Palace before he left it, lest the trying ordeal before him should shake his courage, and a feeling of trepidation on his part shock the national pride. They proceeded to Bamor mounted on thirty richly-caparisoned elephants, and followed by a host of light horsemen with the Mahratta spear in their hands. On arriving they were permitted to take seats on the left hand of the Governor-General, while on the right hand were arrayed Sir Hugh Gough, Mr. Frederick Currie, Colonel Sleeman, and a great number of British officers, all of course in full dress. Lord Ellenborough, habited in the Windsor uniform, then addressed the native audience in a speech of marvellous power, if vehemence be a proof of it. It seemed to us as a capricious prank on the part of Lord Ellenborough to determine on making a sensation-speech to the little Maharajah and his nobles in the English language, as not one word could they understand.

Our language, it has often been remarked, even when spoken by the silvery voice of a Macaulay, is considered to be very unmusical to the foreign ear. But the look, the gestures, and the severe style of a Roman consul, which his Lordship rather too closely imitated on that occasion, were in the last degree unsuitable to native listeners. When they are addressed in their own tongue, they appreciate a lecture, if delivered with the ease and quietness of a friendly preceptor; but it was quite a mistake to imagine Gyajee Scindea to be a juvenile Cataline to be 'whipped' with strong words, or his nobles a factious mob to be scared by them. When his Lordship had concluded, he called on Colonel Sleeman to do the speech again in choice Hindostanee. No one could have been so well qualified if the object had been a mere translation delivered with Oriental propriety. An eminent linguist, he rightly understood, if any man did, by long acquaintance with natives of rank, the tone of voice that was most suitable. A quiet conference would at any time be more impressive than the greatest speech ever heard; the one suits their ascetic habits, the other, even if the oration be in their own language, simply confounds them. They return to their homes with one remark on their lips, which would be, that the Lord-

Sahib has a very hot temper. Colonel Sleeman undertook the task. He exhorted in mild words, Lord Ellenborough had warned in fierce ones; he reproved them in the tone of a pastor, while the Lord emulated Rhadamanthus. The improvement was so distasteful to the Governor-General that he suddenly stopped the distinguished translator, and peremptorily desired him 'to speak out as *he* did.' It is not every man that is so gifted with organs of respiration. The Colonel was not, and he refused to continue a duty which was disapproved. Fortunately, there was sitting by the side of his Lordship a talented personage possessed with stronger power of lungs, and the rest of the speech was hit off with true Ellenborough vigour.

The speech itself was never officially reported. If we may rely on the statement of credible persons who heard it, it was from beginning to end a fine specimen of self-laudation, except, indeed, that his Lordship modestly, but hardly fairly, ascribed to 'the British Government,' which could not by any possibility know anything whatever of what was being done, acts which his own ambition alone had prompted. He began by lauding the gallantry of his troops, and paid due honour to the vast power of the British Government. He denounced the insolence of individuals of the Gwalior Court, and finally dwelt, with great complacency, on the MAGNANIMITY of our Government in restoring to his own throne the Maharajah. Little Gyajee, while this vain extravagance was going on, kept up his mettle by chewing *paun* inordinately, for which early act of heroism under difficulties he was warmly congratulated by the nobles on his return to his Queen-mother. The fate of this poor girl was now to be determined. She was deposed from the regency, and a pension assigned to her, payable, we need scarcely add, out of the Gwalior revenues. Then the Durbar itself, as a political institution, was abolished, and a ministry of five persons was nominated by Lord Ellenborough, which, by the terms of the new treaty, was bound to carry out whatever measures the Resident should direct during the long minority of the Maharajah. Of these registering clerks, two were exiled for life for the most atrocious bribery, one never attended to any business at all, the ordinary transactions of the State being conducted with very great ability by the chief member, Ram Rao Phalkea, who had been minister under the old régime on more than one occasion. Then came measures to consolidate and strengthen British power under the thin disguise of maintaining order. Colonel Orlando Stubbs, a very gallant officer, was nominated Governor of the Fort of Gwalior, a place of high renown in India. In the days of the Delhi Emperors it was the State prison of the empire, on account of its vast strength. Humayoon, the great Mogul, had resided in it; the son of Dara Shikoh was poisoned in one of its dungeons. Tradition carries its history to ages before the birth of our Saviour. It was now to be occupied by British troops, called by courtesy 'Scindea's Own,' and to have a British governor.

But, as we had lost in the battles one general, many good officers, and more than 1,000 valuable lives, it was necessary to show to Lord Ellenborough's adversaries in Parliament more signal advantages than those we have mentioned to compensate for so great and grievous a loss — to no one more grievous than to his Lordship we perfectly well know. There was first a heavy bill of cost: that amounted to 260,000*l.*, and the Durbar was ordered to pay it within fourteen days. It was paid. But that was the least humiliation. The next step was to disband 20,000 Gwalior sepoys, limiting, by the new treaty which was forced on the young Maharajah, the army that was to be kept up for the future to the proportion sanctioned to the petty chieftains of India. Besides 100 guns taken in battle, the Governor-

General ordered a great number of splendid pieces of cannon, which, as the *Burra Jhinsi*, had long been the especial pride of the nation, to be despatched to our arsenal at Agra. He then reorganised and largely increased the Contingent, taking into our own management a good slice of the Gwalior country to defray the expense of it, which was, at the least, 80,000*l*. a year. The Christian generals of Scindea's late army, Jean Baptiste, Jacob, Salvadore, Alexander, as well as the native commandants among the nobles, were thrown out of their commands and employ of every kind. A disbanded soldiery were scattered over the country to prey on helpless villagers, ready, if the day of our own trial should come, to unite against us.

As the real game to be played out by Lord Ellenborough was to disperse Scindea's own army and to place in its stead another, which, while really our own, was falsely to be called Scindea's — as this was to be the crowning incident of the intervention — we proceed to give a brief account of the great Contingent. It numbered 10,000 men of all arms. Maintained at the sole expense of the Maharajah, and called by his name, it was a British force stationed close to his Capital, avowedly to overawe the prince, his court, the five registering clerks who were called ministers, and the people. It far eclipsed, by the splendour of its uniform and fine discipline, every other native force in India, though the men, being young, had not any title to be considered proved soldiers in the field. The sepoys were picked Brahmins and Rajpoots from the Doâb and the Oude provinces, men of stalwart proportions and most haughty carriage. The Grenadier regiment especially, raised by Captain, now Major-General, G. Bruce Michell, was considered the model native corps in India, and no distinguished traveller passed through the Gwalior country without seeing it as a 'lion.' The artillery was admirable. The commands of the batteries were given to young officers of acknowledged military merit — Vincent Eyre, whose name has been rendered imperishable in the annals of England and India by his heroic services in the darkest hour of the rebellion; Frank Turner and John Hall Smyth, whose gallant deeds in 1857 riveted the attention of the House of Commons when Mr. Ross Mangles happily detailed them. An Affghan hero, Sir George Wymer, K.C.B., commanded. So highly esteemed was this Contingent that, when the frightful news reached Mr. Colvin, the Governor of Agra, that Delhi was in possession of the mutineers, he turned his eyes at once to this force for succour, and the far-famed Grenadier regiment, under the command of Major Hennessy, who, when a youth, led 'the forlorn hope' at Bhurtpoor, was sent to Etawah to keep open the high road which connects Delhi to our great arsenal at Allahabad. But this Contingent was, like all the native troops in Bengal, rotten at the core; it entered with alacrity into the great conspiracy, rose at night on its officers, and cruelly butchered all whom they could find. Nevertheless, though the native officers and men were steeped in slaughter, it will ever be remembered in India that they alone, of all the host of mutineers, showed some generalship, and that, in their first encounter with British soldiers, they fairly surprised, destroying the tents of his division and driving him to seek refuge behind the trenches of Cawnpoor, Windham, the hero of the Redan.

It will be seen by and by that this last creation of Lord Ellenborough's was infinitely worse than a very costly failure; but now a fatality was destined to wait on his Lordship himself. HE WAS RECALLED! No event in Indian history caused more astonishment. A little slip of printed paper issued from the Delhi Gazette office, not larger than an ordinary visiting card, and called 'The Express,' announced the news and distracted everybody. It was felt that the most powerful Tory Government since the time of William Pitt was in office, and that its very last intention would be to remove the Duke's especial favourite. Then *who* had done it, and *what* had done it? These enquiries soon ceased to be a matter of doubt. The mail itself arrived, and it was then seen that three elderly gentlemen in Leadenhall Street, called the select committee of the India House, had at last suffered their long pent up indignation to blaze out, and, regardless alike of their own strong conservative tendencies and the severe pressure put upon them by Sir Robert Peel himself, resolved at all costs to avenge their offended dignity by using a power which never before had been exercised, and they, accordingly, with a stroke from a pen, hurled the Autocrat of all India from his imperial throne! It was soon whispered abroad that all his Lordship's 'brothers and sisters,' great and small, young and old, signalled far and wide that the day of universal rejoicing had now broken upon their land.

We have here to remind the reader that a few months ago the London newspapers published a very remarkable despatch from the late Lord Canning to Sir Charles Wood, the Indian Secretary of State, on the subject of ADOPTION as affecting the succession to the native principalities of India. A paragraph of this very interesting State paper is devoted to 'the House of Scindea,' and, as it is curious in showing what misapprehension prevailed in the highest quarter, we transcribe it. Lord Canning, in a former part of this despatch, alluded to 'the haze of doubt' on the subject of adoption, and proceeded to say, 'It is to this alone' (the haze of doubt) 'that I can ascribe the extraordinary satisfaction with which my assurance to Gyajee Scindea, that the Government would see with pleasure his adoption of a successor if lineal heirs should fail him, and that it was the desire of the paramount Power that his house should perpetuate and flourish, was accepted by those attached to his Court;—to the extent that at Gwalior the news was received with rejoicing very like that which would have marked the birth of an heir.' We beg especial attention to what follows:—'For there is not a State which had stronger or more practical proofs of the wish of the British Government that its *integrity* should be maintained than Gwalior; from the time when, in 1826 and 1827, the then Maharajah was in his last illness perseveringly pressed by Lord Amherst to adopt an heir, and was assured that nothing could be further from the wish or intention of the Government than to exercise then and *thereafter any interference in the internal administration of his country*, or to pretend to control the succession to his State, down to 1843, *when the present Maharajah, then a child, was placed upon his throne and confirmed in the possession of it by Lord Ellenborough in person.*'

Anyone would naturally suppose, from this little piece of touching sentimentalism, which was published in 1862, that the State of Gwalior had been, since 1843, in the full enjoyment of that palmy condition of independence which our sympathy with its rights, and our unceasing desire to uphold them, had contributed to form the leading features of our foreign policy in this principality; and that Lord Ellenborough in 1843 could not rest satisfied, on hearing of the death of Junkojee Scindea, with any attention to his successor, Gyajee, which fell short of placing the child on his throne 'in person,' notwithstanding the journey to be undertaken, before that act of his solicitude could be gratified, extended over 700 miles. The only unfortunate thing in this official document is, that, as far as it referred to Scindea, it is entirely imaginative. No one for a moment can possibly doubt that Lord Canning, the noblest and by very far the most popular Governor-

General that ever ruled India, did most implicitly believe every word which he penned. He had simply failed, amid a multiplicity of anxious duties, to enquire into all the facts, and had a very careless foreign-secretary to guide him. Its inaccuracy is abundantly tested by the little fact that Gyajee Scindea was placed on the throne in February 1843, and that Lord Ellenborough had not set his foot on Gwalior territory until the following December. It will of course excite surprise and regret to find that so great a Governor-General as Lord Canning was should have written, that 'nothing had been further from the wish or intention of the British Government than to exercise any interference in the internal administration of Gwalior,' when we know that Lord Ellenborough had disbanded its army; taken away its guns; abolished, as a political institution, the Durbar; nominated its ministry, to which no independent action was allowed; and forced, by the point of the bayonet, a treaty on the State, by the terms of which its power was for ever limited in respect of the enlistment of its soldiery. That Lord Canning's proclamation gave rise to manifestations of public joy is no matter for wonder, but their true cause escaped his acute mind. There had never been any 'haze of doubt' at Gwalior in regard to 'adoption,' but a very thick haze as concerned our proceedings, wishes, and intentions, which was dispelled by our Queen's promise, which no viceroy will, the people knew, dare to break. Hence the joy! Lord Ellenborough rarely cared to veil his motives, so we find him stating in 1843, before he set out on his visit to Gyajee Scindea, 'that to maintain unimpaired the position which we now hold in India is a duty, not to ourselves alone, but to humanity. The adoption of new views of policy'—that policy which the mutinies of 1857 taught us was the only safe one—'weakness under the name of moderation, and pusillanimity under that of forbearance, would not avert from our own territory the evils we let loose upon India; and the only result of false measures would be, to remove the scene of a contest, altogether inevitable, from Gwalior to Allahabad, there to be carried on with diminished force, a disheartened army, and a disaffected people.' It was only a very short period after that revelation of his views, when Lord Ellenborough mounted his war-horse, and advanced his armies on Gwalior.

We now return to the year 1844. It is not our intention to detail the ordinary occurrences of a native Capital controlled by British troops during the long minority of its prince. The Ellenborough ministers of course adhered to the stipulations of the Ellenborough convention; they put on a significant grin, perhaps, when their old acquaintances at court congratulated them on the departed glory of their Raj. There were in the city the same buzz and bustle, and here and there one man might be heard recounting to another the variety of sash, epaulette, and helmet in the Lord-Sahib's beautiful Contingent hard by. The general aspect of affairs, in a word, was monotonous, and if the expression may be allowed, most painfully tranquil. Whenever a noble was reported contumacious, a letter from the Supreme Government intimated to him that a continuance in such a course of conduct would lead to perpetual imprisonment in *our* penal fortress of Chunar. No measures for the better administration of the country were introduced, the intention being to alter as little as possible, but 'to establish visibly our influence.' Such seemed to be the first results of our intervention, and the only ones indeed, year after year, that came to our knowledge.

We had occasion elsewhere to remark, that the native princes, excepting now and then they might reckon on a traditionary old Indian of the Malcolm and Metcalfe school, had not a friend among the members of the two services or the press of India;

and now that we, passing over many years, are coming to the period of the mutinies, it is necessary to add, that the great organ of public intelligence in England entertained still less sympathy for them. On the 22nd of August, 1857, a time when the people of England, shocked beyond the power of language to describe by the recent news of the massacre of women and children at Delhi, looked with the deepest anxiety for the arrival of the next steamer, to learn if the defection of the native army had become general, a telegram announced the alarming fact, that both Scindea's and Holkar's magnificent Contingents had risen and murdered their officers. The next day 'The Times' opened its heaviest battery, and cannonaded these luckless princes in the following vigorous manner:—

'As to the conduct of Holkar and the Gwalior Chief, and of their Contingents, it was precisely what was to be expected. The Chiefs profess loyalty, and are wholly unable to give us the only proof of it by the loyalty of their men. To us it is a matter of minor importance whether the Chiefs themselves stand by us or not. They may or may not be in earnest. If they are, then it is evident they possess not a shadow of authority, and the sooner they cease to encumber territories which they cannot control the better for the general good. If they are not in earnest, if their Contingents know very well that their offence is not unpardonable, then their Chiefs are only pursuing the common Indian policy of consulting appearances and personal safety as long as possible, though it be at the expense of truth.' *

At this distant period, it is difficult to imagine the feeling of indignation excited against these princes by that crushing article. Presently we shall show that their conduct justly established between themselves and the Queen's Government a bond of gratitude which no time, let us hope, can break. But the error that 'The Times' fell into was by no means a ludicrous one. Every urchin in our streets knows very well that a horse-chestnut is not a chestnut horse, but the greatest intellect of ephemeral literature might be excused for not understanding that Scindea's Contingent was not the Contingent of 'the Gwalior Chief.' In name, it fraudulently was. As matter of fact, it simply gave the very best illustration of a new and expressive parliamentary term, 'an organised hypocrisy.' It was a gigantic imposition.

Let us consider how the Chiefs 'consulted appearances.' Five miles from Indore, Holkar's capital, we had two native regiments. They mutinied at

* *The Times*' leader, August 23, 1857.

parade and butchered their respective Commandants and Adjutants, who alone were on the ground. The other officers, unable to render any assistance, hearing volley after volley of musketry, fled to the fort, an old dilapidated building at Mhow. Holkar, as soon as he heard of the catastrophe, despatched his own soldiers, themselves thirsting for Christian blood, and saved their lives. Afterwards, in our distress, he placed his own treasure at the disposal of the British Government. That is what one of the wily Barons did who 'encumbered a territory' in a remote part of India, and where no other aid was possible. And what did the other Baron? Pressed by his enraged subjects to declare for the King of Delhi, arguing, as they well might, that the name alone of Scindea would rally to his standard the whole warlike Hindoo populations of Central India—the Jauts and the Rajpoots—and that the Mahratta race in the Dekhan would follow, he sacrificed ambition; declined to be made a hero; restrained the impatience of his subjects by vague promises; betrayed to Major Macpherson, the British agent at his Court, the revelations of the emissaries of the leading rebels; warned that able officer of the intention of the Gwalior Contingent to rise, a fact the bare suspicion of which the officers for a long time indignantly repudiated offered to throw open one of his palaces to our affrighted ladies and children in the cantonments, an offer accepted one day, but which, through a fatal return of confidence, was relinquished the next; and when the night of slaughter did come, as earnestly and repeatedly foretold by him it would, he conveyed all the Officers who contrived to escape, in his own carriages, under the safe escort of his body-guard, to Agra. These were, however, the earliest and not the most important of his services. At least, we ascribe to his readiness of resource, after the British agent had left him, and when a host of Christians were crowded together within the walls of the fortress of Agra, the greatest service which he rendered to our cause. Delhi was still in the possession of the rebels, and so desperate did our chance of success then appear that wise men suggested to the Governor-General to parley with the King's confidential agents. What if, at that critical period, the most renowned fortress of India, whose magnificent walls of red sandstone overtop the second city of the old Mahommedan dynasty, also fell! The Engineer in charge had anxiously examined the place, and formed the opinion that the heavy guns of the Gwalior Contingent, if brought to bear on its walls, would certainly open a breach. It was known that the Nusseerabad and Neemuch brigades had mutinied, and were moving up to Agra, and the most reflective of our officers thought it probable that the Gwalior Contingent would also push on, join these men at Dholepoor on the Chumbul, and march together on Agra. The subtle artifice of Scindea, guided no doubt by the judgment of his most able Minister, Dinker Rao, saved Agra; perhaps—who can say?—our Indian empire. To convince his people that he was no longer attached to what was now regarded at his Capital as a fallen cause, he prevailed on Major Macpherson to leave his country. He then set to work to detain the Contingent at Gwalior. Fortunately for us, the men had 'looted' our treasury to the amount of 50,000*l.*, and were not very anxious for immediate field service. Indeed, after their fury had been expended on the Christians, they calmed down and began to look out for a leader. They elected the Subadar Major of the Grenadier Regiment, Amanut Ally, and conferred on him the modest rank of General-in-Chief! He was, it is true, a fine old soldier, but having already served the Company with zeal and distinction over fifty years, he was not quite that sort of presiding genius which was wanted to hound his men on to conquest. Whether he indulged in the expectation of seizing Agra, we cannot affirm, but this we do know, that he was unable to prevent two of his regiments from going over to Scindea, and no doubt was entertained that all the rest would be alienated from his authority by the tempting offers of the prince. Thus, by means of one subterfuge or other, the Contingent remained three months inactive at Gwalior, by which time Agra was relieved, and all danger had passed away. These were, then, the transcendent services of a Chief who 'encumbered a territory, and consulted appearances, and his own personal safety as long as possible.' A matter of reproach to this chivalrous youth, who braved the furious throng that besieged his palace, disregarded the entreaties of the zenana, turned with disbelief from his priests, resolving at any cost to stand or fall with the British Government! That cost was indeed great.

By this time it was seen clearly enough that Scindea's promises were delusive. The people and the army thereupon became overbearing, and opened communications with Tantia Topee, the Nana's lieutenant-general, who presently arrived at Gwalior. The prince found himself deserted. An attempt was made to seize him, and, finding his orders disobeyed and himself left to the mercy of a few horsemen who attended him, he fled to Agra. As soon as his flight was made known, his palaces were pillaged, and a relation of the Nana was formally enthroned on the 'silken cushion' of this Mahratta State. We must not quite lose sight, at this perilous moment, of our old acquaintance Amanut Ally, General-in-Chief. After enduring every sort of indignity from the hands of those who had made him a General, he also escaped, taking refuge in the city of Gwalior where he lay concealed until the Contingent marched for Cawnpoor to look after Windham. He remained there till our troops, some months afterwards, drove Tantia Topee and his rabble out of Gwalior, and then, with incredible infatuation, he commenced a round of visits to the British officers of the force! Meade, an officer whose gallantry during the mutinies was most conspicuous, happening to hear of Amanut Ally's attentions, caused him to be apprehended and conveyed to Agra for trial. It appeared in evidence that the very first act of this General-in-Chief, on assuming his command, was to indite a letter to 'the Protector of the World,' the King of Delhi, expressive of his detestation of his old master, John Company, and of his very high satisfaction in having already sent many Christians to ——! This interesting document, signed by the wretch, was found in the palace at Delhi, and, to his dismay, was brought forth at the trial; yet, strange to add, efforts were made to save his life. In fact, he was not so black as he chose to make 'the Protector of the World' believe. Being in command of some troops at Etawah at the break-out in that station, he used his influence to save the lives of twenty Christians, who were utterly at the mercy of his men. He now asked, in return, for mercy; but to ask for mercy in that day was as vain as to preach to the wind. When the old man perceived that all hope of life was gone, he drew himself up to his full height, and thus addressed the Court: 'Sahib logue (gentlemen), I see that I am not to be forgiven—that my life is gone; but, because I served your Government for more than fifty years, save me from disgrace. Let a few of your Europeans shoot me. Do not hang me.' The request, however, was not heeded, and he was hanged.

The city of Gwalior having, during Scindea's absence, become a perfect pandemonium, the wealthy classes looked forward with joy at the approach of a British army to restore their prince and to burst the thraldom that had so heavily afflicted them since his exile. Even the people, whose arbitrary bearing had been so openly displayed on account of his loyalty to us, could not crush or squeeze enough to get a sight of him. The hordes of rebels under Tantia Topee, whose successes were at this period the amazement of all India, were driven by their fears into the dense jungles of Malwa and Bundlekhund, carrying with them the immense plunder of the palaces and treasury of Gwalior. We find Gyajee Scindea, then, again seated on 'the silken cushion' of his ancestors, if not the most popular of Mahratta princes—for an anti-English feeling is not eradicated from the public mind by unsuccessfulness—yet with far more certainty of handing down to his children, and his children's children, the hereditary possessions of his remarkable House, than had any chieftain of his line since the days of Sevajee; subject, however, to the grievous loss of that independence which the unjust aggression of 1843 effected, and which still excites the secret indignation of our most faithful ally and friend. Perhaps even yet a generous consideration may induce the Queen's Government to enquire into all the circumstances which actuated the strange proceedings of Lord Ellenborough, and to ascertain 'the reason why' the independence of this State was forfeited on such a wretched pretext as that which was advanced—'to avoid removing the scene of a contest, altogether inevitable, from Gwalior to Allahabad, there to be carried on with diminished force, a disheartened army, and a disaffected people.' To us this reads like mere hallucination—the wanderings of a disquieted mind; yet it was, on this shallow reasoning alone, deemed just and proper to disarm the State, throw down the walls of its Fortress, strip the Capital of its guns, and to confine, within a certain limit, its power to enlist a soldier. Possibly, the earnest advocate for the Poles, now that his ears are no longer open to the adulations of his armies, may assist to repair the injuries which his own hand inflicted.

In concluding this slight sketch at the period when the Maharajah was restored to his throne, we will venture a passing remark or two on the main cause of the great mutinies. The sole object of the mutineers was of course the overthrow of British power in India, and that purpose was frustrated, not by one miracle, but by 'a succession of miracles.' The principal cause was the hateful and monstrous practice of annexation, which was nothing else than the total subversion of the rights and property of the upper classes of the State; and, in respect to Oude, the destruction, also, of the peculiar privileges of the sepoys of that immense native army which mainly upheld the empire. Now that the transfer of the Government has been completely effected, the time has arrived when the whole truth may be written, albeit the revelation may be disagreeable. The system, like that of Thuggee, Dacoitee, Slavery, Infanticide, has happily, let us hope, departed for ever. It was, in almost every instance since 1830, except in that of the Punjaub, the gratification of ambition on the part of the Governor-General, and neither the work nor the desire of the East India Direction, which, let what may be alleged against it, was ever more regardful of the rights of its princes and people, than of mere selfish considerations. An Earl's coronet, or the one higher than that in dignity, was the sure reward on the return of the 'brilliant annexationist' to England. But the sapping and mining part of the operation necessarily fell to the lot of the Resident, without whose active aid little could be done. If that powerful functionary were a Cavendish, as was the case at Gwalior in 1834, when that State was *avowedly* coveted with a view 'to connect the territory of Agra to that of Bombay;' or a Outram in Scinde, when, as in 1843, there was a craving for the free navigation of the Indus; or a Mansel at Nagpoor, when it was seen that the splendid cotton districts would open a new source of wealth, then the attempts at seizure would for a time break down. It would be deemed necessary to find a pretext for his removal, putting into his place an individual of high character and great repute, but whose idiosyncrasy was known to be a peculiar capacity to play the part of an accomplished *detective.* Of course it is very ungracious to say this, and we tell it lowly. Court bulletins next follow. The native parasites of the great man accompany their master in his morning and evening walks, and soon earn their welcome by their marvellous revelations. The character and the habits of the Chief are depicted by those amusing hangers-on, and their account is sedulously kept before the eye of the British public by the Resident. The nobles are 'robber-chiefs;' the army is 'disorganised.' We never knew a native army, except our own sepoy one, that was not at some time or other said to be 'mutinous,' 'insolent,' and 'oppressive.' Then, though 'the wrongs of the people' were beyond endurance, it was seriously alleged that nobody in the State possessed the power to enforce the execution of a single order. The frontiers were of course in disorder; and the universal oppression was intolerable. These statements were followed up by 'friendly' remonstrances; very mild ones if the hot winds prevailed, as a long period must intervene before British troops could be employed; stronger in the rain-season, when the disposition of our army is arranged; and very potent ones at the approach of the cold season, when our troops are ready for any emergency.

Then it is that with 'great reluctance' the Governor-General proceeds to take possession. There was one Viceroy who, if he did not with his own hands set the State-traps, yet contrived to have them so dexterously set by his Residents, that he caught a Principality year after year, as surely as the cold season came round; but such is the astonishing popularity of his memory, such the fame of his 'brilliant' administration, that if we ventured to name him, we should be regarded by a host of his admirers with incredulous horror ever afterwards. Sometimes, though not very often, the Resident stopped short, and refused to be a party to the felony, as when the annexation of Oude was near at hand, Sir William Sleeman told the Governor-General 'that such an act of spoliation would cost the British Government more than the value of ten such kingdoms, and would inevitably lead to the mutiny of the great Indian army. The seizure of that garden of India cost us more than a hundred such kingdoms were worth, for it led to the massacre of our officers, their wives, and their children; the expenditure of many millions; the loss of our prestige; and the undying hatred between race and race.